CH00842211

TRANSITION

TRANSITION

A compass for shifting from the old to the new featuring key areas of reformation for the post-charismatic kingdom saint

Servant Robin

TRANSITION

Copyright © 2012 Robin Jegede-Brimson
No part of this book may be reproduced or transmitted in any form or by any means, electronic, mechanical, photocopying and recording or by any information storage and retrieval system without the written permission from the author. All scripture quotations are taken from the King James Version of the Holy Bible.

7th edition
Published by
SERVANT BOOKS (www.servantministries.co.uk)

Distributed by
Robin Jegede-Brimson
Servant Ministries
7, Belton Close, Whitstable, Kent
CT5 4LG, UK
+44(0) 787 202 4364
GodsOyster@aol.com

AFRICA
Henry Hamilton
Servant Ministries Nigeria
U.I.P.O. Box 22974, Ibadan, Nigeria.
+234(0) 80 3368 1552.
hamiltonh78@hotmail.com

Cover design by
BARLT GRAPHICS PRINTS, NIG.
+234(0) 70 3822 8234
barltprints@gmail.com

"Men of Issachar, who understood the
times and knew what
Israel ought to do"

1Chronicles 12:32

To U* The HOLY SPIRIT, my companion and first love

ENDORSEMENTS

Robin has provided us with an extremely important and well thought-through update on the trends that are presently evident as God is constantly renewing His Church. It is commendable that he has done this with real respect for God's three-generational pattern. As the spiritual fathers and mothers among us read this they will be reminded of how God used them to bring change in their younger days and will be inspired to add their weight to God's ongoing spiritual momentum. As today's spiritual children read this they will be encouraged to reach out for constant freshness in their developing ministries. For the generation, however, that is currently tasked with driving things forward there is a spiritual imperative not to hold back but to push ahead with enthusiasm and determination, trusting God to sanctify their endeavours with His humility and grace. May we all be empowered to embrace God's ever-transitioning agenda for renewal.

Hugh Osgood
Co-Chair, The UK Charismatic and Pentecostal Conference. Chair, Churches in Communities

The joyful expectation in the Holy Spirit of what lies ahead gives us the zeal to face another day! This book teaches us how the Holy Spirit is enabling saints to break free from every limitation into a life of restoration and abundance. The thief comes to steal, kill and to destroy but Jesus Christ came to give us life and life abundantly. As you journey with Robin Jegede-Brimson in this book, you will see the Holy Spirit take you to new level in God.

Bishop Joe Ibojie
Senior Pastor & Best Selling Author
The Father's House
Aberdeen, Scotland

I love Robin's heart for Jesus. His unabashed passion for Jesus' mission undeniable and inspiring

Jim Denison
Team Leader, Canterbury Vineyard

A man's words hold no more value than his character. If his character is not good, I have a very difficult time hearing his words. Robin is a man of God that I have had the opportunity to spend considerable with. Not only with him, but his family also - wife, children, and parents. He is a man of character in the home and away from the home; with his wife, with his children, and with his parents. He has a hunger for God, he is a man of prayer, and he has the fire of God within. He is one that I would not hesitate to read what he has to say.

He listens for the voice of God and carefully speaks as not to say the wrong words. He is not a man of arrogance but one of humility and of a teachable spirit. I recommend his writings based on the strength of character that he possesses. I know they have come from a heart of hunger to edify the body of Christ.

John Bailey
Evangelist and Missionary USA / Philippines

Knowing your call and where you fit into the jigsaw of ministry is a depth many Christian believers never grasp. Having worked and walked with Robin over 20 odd years has convinced me, he has found his place in ministry. Robin is a voice to this generation and it is a clear tone with which he declares the prophetic call. Humbled to say I have learnt a lot from him.

Pastor Tunde Babalola
National Officer, Church Planting, RCCG, Ireland

Robin has been my friend of about 30 years. I have known Robin to be a man of passion for God and great pursuits after God. We have shared together great seasons of worship and prayer exploits. In this book, Robin shares from all this wealth of experiences and I believe you will be greatly imparted as you read.

Michael Oludipe
Pastor, New Covenant Church, Manchester

Robin has been spending time in the presence of the Almighty. He has been sitting at Jesus feet and he has been taking notes. His subsequent book TRANSITION looks forward to where Father is leading His Church, whilst honouring the past and honestly facing present day realities. It is a valuable addition to what many are sensing the Spirit is saying to the Church, helping to bring otherwise abstract thoughts and ideas into sharper focus. Although TRANSITION is a relatively short book, take your time, it is packed with insights that will make you want to pause for deeper reflection and prayer. Like all good prophecy, it pushes you towards Father and doesn't do all the work for you. I highly recommend you read it at least twice, prayerfully considering its message whilst spending your own quality time in His presence.

Norman
Kent Prayer Journeys

CONTENTS

ACKNOWLEDGEMENTS & APPRECIATION

I owe many mighty men and women of GOD gratitude for all their input into my life as well as into the continuing worldwide reformation.

IN NIGERIA

My thanks to Rev (Dr) Paul Jinudu, leader of the worldwide New Covenant Church, one of the first apostles I met as a young Christian in 1981, needless to say his first few messages are indelibly printed on my heart.

In my quest for 'What was to come' I am thankful for the missionary apostle, Pa S G Elton who on the back of a prophetic word, left the comforts of Bradford in England for the unknown town of Ilesa, Nigeria in 1931. From there he discipled a whole array of apostles across Nigeria up until his call to glory in January 1987. It was my privilege to visit and receive counsel from him several times as a young student.

I am immensely grateful to Rev Olubi Johnson who broke out of the box as a result of his vision for a new breed of what was to be a trendy charismatic church in Ibadan, Nigeria in 1983. This was at a time when no one knew what this would look like, it was made up as we journeyed. I remember to my delight that apart from there being excellent teaching, that the ladies were permitted to wear make up in his church! Many global leaders have stemmed from this church.

As he was being raised up others in Lagos, Nigeria like Pastor Tunde Joda were also receiving this new wine and having encounters with heaven and pressing on in faith for what they had dreamt about. Rev (Dr) Francis Wale Oke, also in Ibadan was ordained and commissioned along with three others by Archbishop Benson Idahosa into ministry. Benson Idahosa was then the foremost forerunner into the new style churches as early as the mid 70's, he too was a disciple of Pa S.G. Elton. From his spiritual loins came other giants like Pastor Chris Oyakhilome, a very famous international preacher with a massive worldwide church movement.

In 1981 I met another leader who The LORD used to shape my concept of prayer, of humility and several other things; Pastor Enoch Adeboye of the world wide, Redeemed Christian Church of GOD which has grown to host some of the largest prayer meetings in the world, often numbering in excess of one million people! I was intrigued by the modalities for the release of The SPIRIT by an another apostle, Rev Yemi Ayodele. He brought a release of The SPIRIT of GOD into the hearts of those being rapidly saved and birthed into this then new charismatic move.

As young believers we knew something new was being placed on our shoulders, we were so hungry

and thirsty for knowledge, The LORD raised up a teaching apostle, Emiko Amotsuka to satisfy our thirst, he began to bring in books and magazines on faith and the gifts of The HOLY SPIRIT from Kenneth E Hagin in America. His seminars were "must attend" events and impacted a generation of Nigerians.

I also have to thank William Kumuyi, who like so many leaders of the 70's began what are now mega church wine skins from the humble surrounds of their sitting rooms. His church, the Deeper Life Bible Church quickly caught the heart of GOD for the nations and had missions all over Africa by the mid 80's - a time when the charismatic move was still in it's infancy in many parts.

The FATHER was not only raising church planting apostles, he was also calling out missionary apostles. Reuben Ezemadu of Christian Missionary Foundation imparted much to me about the heart for the worlds unreached peoples.

There were prophets with a mantle to teach on prayer and raise strategic prayer initiatives that would ensure the movement pressed into its zenith, I am thankful for meeting Emeka Nwankpa as well as Steve Olumuyiwa, founding fathers of Intercessors for Nigeria and Africa.

Appreciation

I am grateful to Rev (Dr) Moses Aransiola who has taken 'Prayer Schools' to the nations and ushered in an emphasis on prayer.

As I trace those I wish to acknowledge and appreciate I go into the early 90's. Soon after this first wave of churches from the 80's another wave began to hit the spiritual climate of Nigeria. A minister was called to come south from Kaduna in Nigeria and establish 'a people' in Lagos the commercial capital; he broke traditional dress codes by wearing a native flowing robe to preach (agbada), he was decidedly different. In the space of a couple of decades Pastor David Oyedepo of Winners Chapel fulfilled his call to raise a people and now has the largest auditorium in the world. He was raised on the shoulders of Benson Idahosa and charismatic leaders in the USA like Kenneth Hagin and Kenneth Copeland.

As the 80's merged into the 90's another wave came in from America to energize the movement– the Full Gospel Business Men's Fellowship aka The Happiest People on Earth! Through this movement The HOLY SPIRIT broke through from the common people to the ruling classes of the nation in Nigeria. Bankers, lawyers, doctors, business people were swept in to the church. Tunde Jaiyebo and Femi Emmanuel were some of the young visionaries GOD used, I am grateful for the opportunities to meet with them and their input into my life.

These were among the leaders of this new movement who raised disciples, taking this 'new wine' and its emphasis on tongues, liberty in worship and financial and physical wholeness into the towns of southern Nigeria! We owe you all so much. What a mighty platform GOD used you to build for the charismatic movement!

WORLDWIDE

We soon began to realise that this new move was not restricted to Nigeria alone, men were being raised in Ghana like Duncan Williams and Mensa Otabil. In America we had people like Joel Osteen, Morris Cerullo and Creflo Dollar teaching us the basics of new found truths from GOD's word.

In the UK, we became aware of men like Colin Dye of Kensington Temple, which was then the place to go in London in the 80's. New movements were birthed in the 70's and 80's around father-figure apostles. Terry Virgo (New Frontiers Int'l), Barney Coombs (Salt and Light), Colin Urqhuart (Kingdom Faith) & Roger Forster (Ichthus).

Wow! How can we ever thank all these generals enough?

Then I must thank some of my favourite authors, Bill Hamon, C Peter Wagner, Rick Joyner (must read book is *Final Quest*) and John Eckhardt (*Moving in the Apostolic*) whose writings I have for devoured especially on the apostolic, the saints movement and prophetic ministry.

Come the 21st century another section of people were being released on the world stage – Bill Johnson (*How heaven invades Earth*), Danny Silk (must read book is *Culture of Honour*), Patricia King and David Herzog.

Some of these authors are taking the church even deeper into something that seems to transcend the charismatic movement. For lighting a way beyond what I have been privileged to see I must also thank you. I cannot fail to mention and thank other leading lights in my search for the 'new move', all whom have helped tremendously to keep my wine skin soft - Catherine Brown, Heidi Baker (one of the most passionate women on the planet!), Steve Shultz (whose Elijah list mailings shed incredible light!) as well as Trevor & Sharon Baker. My thanks to Pete Carter (Eastgate) whose school of the supernatural blessed me and freed me to be me. My quest to be a father has been powerfully modelled by Michael Puffet (Jubilee Church, Maidstone), thanks.

A special thanks to Cheryl Fritz and all my friends at Inside Out Prophetic, an excellent online training school for all things prophetic using skype as a medium of communication; I learnt so much here.

Coming closer home I'd like to thank my friend Jim Dennison for modelling in Canterbury (Canterbury

Vineyard) what we need to see more of - thanks buddy. I cannot fail to mention my closest friend in Whitstable, Martin Bentley for journeying with me for the last 16 years. Then again I thank Ben & Joan White who caught the rain of the HOLY SPIRIT and built a community of believers with it in Whitstable in the 80's. Also appreciation to Richard Ferrant and Phil Hulks who as teenagers in Herne Bay some 30 years ago sought to model a wine skin that would both receive and release the new charismatic wine. You have leaped through one movement right into the next! I would like to thank my closest friends Michael "Schamach" Oludipe as well as Richard Mitchell, who models for me what it is to be a mentoring apostle-prophet. Nelson Adetuberu is among the emerging prophets in my home nation, he demonstrates how to flow along with The HOLY SPIRIT.

Thanks to my wife, Nyema for carrying on with all 'the stuff' essential to daily living while I spent time on this. To Henry Hamilton, a hidden gem about to be exposed for working behind the scenes to support me with this as well as my other books. My appreciation to Paul & Monica, Mum & Dad for partnering with me on this project. Love you Nyema, thank you for letting me adventure in GOD!

Appreciation

PREFACE

Times and seasons. Periods of change. Eras in which we are called to build on what has been attained by previous moves. Each new season calls for a change in emphasis in our quest to build the church as well as to fulfil the great commission. As we glance back at history we can see clearly the hand of GOD on different people at different times. Using His sons and daughters to gently and lovingly shepherd His people higher and deeper in revelation, into divine truths and knowledge once hidden, but now revealed. Revealed so we can all now walk in those once mysterious truths! What an honour for us to enter into what knowledge is now freely available. We have been so mightily blessed by chosen instruments whose very lives now come to represent essential truths to us. As a result of this the church has moved in leaps and bounds over the last few decades.

A CALM DISQUIET

But for many there has been a sense of a lull, a quiet, almost a sense of stagnation, of beginning to sit into traditions that were once new to us but now are often mere rituals. The danger of a ritual is found in the question, "What aspect of the life of the spirit, might that ritual be in danger of stifling?" We don't want change for the sake of it – just to shake things up a bit. No, that would be daft, but we do want the change that is instituted by The Fresh breath of GOD. And one of the ways

that this will often happen is by our being willing to muck about a bit and do things differently, more naturally and less 'religiously' - it may come as a surprise to some of us that The SPIRIT does not like religion. 'Religion' - set ways and patterns that have become institutionalised.

So those who are seeking for change and are feeling a restless disquiet within them are poised at the brink of a new thing happening on the earth. And true to form, The HOLY SPIRIT has been speaking and introducing several notable paradigm shifts. Changes that The Body of Christ is being called to undergo, to make the transition from the era of the charismatic move and into a 'new wine' 'Kingdom Saints' release upon the earth.

Can we fix dates to either the charismatic move or to the take off of this new, 'new move'? Yes, by looking down the history lane I feel we can. A good place to start may be by first offering an explanation to the difference between the terms 'Pentecostal' and 'Charismatic'.

TERMS AND DATES
Pentecostalism refers to the first move of The HOLY SPIRIT that began early in the 20th century, which occurred across the world. It was most

notably seen in the Welsh Revival in Europe and the Azusa Street Revival in the USA. Much less

documented is the same movement that occurred across Africa under Simon Kimbangu in the Congo and Joseph Babalola and others in Nigeria. The Pentecostal Movement gave rise to new denominations like the Assemblies of GOD, the Apostolic Church and the Foursquare Gospel Church to name a few. It did not however infiltrate the ranks of pre-existing denominations.

The charismatic movement occurred in two phases, the decades are largely the same but with slightly different settings across the continents.

1ST PHASE: PREPARING THE GROUND 1960 ONWARDS

THE USA AND THE UK

The first phase in the western world began around figures like David DuPlessis aka 'Mr Pentecost', a white south African, who received the baptism of the HOLY SPIRIT and began to share it in mainline denominations across America and Europe. Also in America Demos Shakarian was used to found the FGBMFI, which took the Baptism of The HOLY SPIRIT to business and marketplace leaders. Jean Darnell was a person who impacted England for two decades from 1967 onwards. She fanned the flames of this first phase of charismatic revival. My Mum got saved under her ministry in 1983.

WEST AFRICA

In the African nations particularly Nigeria and Ghana, the move of The HOLY SPIRIT was

confined mostly to the post primary schools and institutions. There they carried the nicknames of SU (after the Scripture Union) or FCS (Fellowship of Christian Students). It was characterised more by a hunger for the truths of the Bible then charismatic gifts.

2ND PHASE: EMERGING WINE SKINS 1970'S & 1980'S ONWARDS

Across both continents we can trace the rise of apostolic leaders whose ministries formed new wine skins in the 70's. This decade saw the start of new house church meetings which in turn led to a new movement. It is reasonable to assume that for this wine to not be wasted, new wine skins needed to ultimately be formed.

As this movement progressed new waves of the HOLY SPIRIT brought in different social classes of people and were followed by new church groupings in the 80's and 90's. These new waves of The SPIRIT softened the hearts of the leaders of traditional denominations who then began to also drink from this new wine.

The HOLY SPIRIT is not confined to dates but these are a guide for us looking at things from an

earthly perspective. He moves in response to our hunger; when HE is about to move afresh He puts hunger into our hearts!

PERSPECTIVES

So, as we collectively pray and prepare for what lies ahead I would like to share a few perspectives. This is in the hope that these will cause a greater preparation for that which is to come. The majority of these points I have gleaned in my travels, reading & searching as I have continued to seek Papa-GOD for new wine in the period from April 2008 to April 2011, an interlude in which I was led by The LORD to lay down ministry work and be free to seek HIM.

For those of us who have observed the charismatic move we can see that there are many things that it has restored to The Body of Christ. Most apparent of these are the office of a pastor, freedom in worship and openness in prayer. But many carry a sense that The Kingdom needs to be given room to expand beyond our church meetings. Yes, we have known how to bring down The SPIRIT & Power of GOD, now we must learn to take it forward. Every move of GOD can be also viewed as a stepping-stone for the next. So we long to see other ministry graces come to the fore. We long to see not just churches multiply in a nation but also the core values of a people change too. We are thankful for many of the truths that have been expounded by the charismatic movement but we are also mindful of the fact that any truth over-emphasised can itself lead to error. When one move becomes jaded and falters in it's momentum it is time to ask The

FATHER the question, 'LORD, is there more?' This book is hopefully about the more.

40-YEAR EPOCHS

It is interesting the many times that the period '40' years is referred to in the scriptures. It speaks of a probationary period also a time of [1]judgement or the [2]chastisement of sons. It can also refer to a [3]transitional time between governments. Many of the OT Judges like [4]Othniel, Ehud, Deborah and Barak as well as [5]Saul and then [6]David and [7]Solomon were all given 40-year tenures of rulership. I feel that prophetically the charismatic movement is just gone 40 years, wow! Something new is on the way!

---

[1] Luke 7:4
[2] Luke 4:2
[3] 1 Kings 19:8
[4] Judges 3:11, 30, 5:31
[5] 1Samuel 13:1
[6] 2Samuel 5:4
[7] 2Chronicles 9:30

I believe that The Bride of CHRIST is called to shift her practise and 'doctrinal posture' in numerous areas. My prayer is that as we do so may we find deeper communion with The HOLY SPIRIT and an

attendant greater effectiveness in our assignments on the earth.

It is mostly about emphasis, what we know to be true by fresh revelation and so realise that we need to focus on to move forwards.

I start with a summary of over thirty key areas where I feel that transition is key. We then in the confines of this book focus on five of these areas – The Trinity, Worship & GOD's Presence, The Gift of Prophecy, The Office of the Prophet & that of the Apostle.

Happy reading!

Love, Joy & Peace,

Robin Jegede-Brimson
Whitstable, Kent
October 2016

Preface

CHAPTER 1
New Wine

He told them this parable: "No one tears a patch from a new garment and sews it on an old one. If he does, he will have torn the new garment, and the patch from the new will not match the old. And no one pours new wine into old wineskins. If he does, the new wine will burst the skins, the wine will run out and the wineskins will be ruined. No, new wine must be poured into new wineskins. And no one after drinking old wine wants the new, for he says, 'The old is better.'"
Luke 5:36 – 39

'NEW WINE'

The LORD JESUS introduced the phrase, 'New Wine' in response to a complaint by the disciples of John the Baptist. The disciples had observed that they seemed to be bearing the brunt of self-sacrifice by fasting often while JESUS's disciples were feasting and merry making! (Matthew 9:14-17)

Historically, new moves are built on the sacrifice and labours of the old. We enjoy the freedom to read and freely obtain numerous editions of the Bible because forerunners like John Wycliffe, John Hus and William Tyndale all paid the ultimate sacrifice to strive for this liberty. Ana-Baptists paid with being drowned in rivers to pay for our freedom to baptise by immersion. Pentecostals suffered martyrdom and were left to rot in lunatic asylums to secure our liberty to be baptised in The Spirit. The list goes on. How does this affect the view from where we are?

HONOURING PREVIOUS MOVES OF GOD

Firstly, we learn to not despise the 'old moves', I have often heard 'new wine' ministers speak disparagingly of the 'faith movement' or outpourings of The SPIRIT being tagged as being 'part GOD, part flesh, part devil'. Ouch! Truth be told, in fresh moves, the new revelations we receive are very often carried to an extreme, this being an obvious reaction to what we are trying to 'fix'. This is not new. Rather than ridicule our "holiness brethren", the "prosperity" move, or wherever our lineage is from, we must learn to acknowledge their labours and sacrifice. Their struggles are what have enabled us to walk in greater freedom and so press on with newer things. We honour their sacrifice; we esteem their labours. We thank them.

Secondly, to those who have run the race before us, it may now appear that 'the gospel' has become soft and we do not 'fast' as often as they did, please forgive this impression, the new is always able to relish the liberties of that which has been won through hardship. In time the 'new' will also face their own forms of persecution as they run their own race, having built on what's been obtained. In so doing the 'new' too will also 'fast' as they press into the fullness of the land they are called to win; this ultimately becoming a legacy to the next generation. Remember - the generation to come will also 'fast', but not as we see now see it. Let's hold our traditions firmly, but with tender hearts and soft hands.

CALLED TO TRANSITION

Entering the second decade of the 21st century, The Body of Christ is being called to process what may be several steep learning curves. This is a necessary condition to Heaven releasing the very best of the wines yet to be poured out on the Earth. This journey will include transitions in how we do church, how we perceive ourselves as believers, how we operate in the world and in the identity of present day saints. The subsequently emerging 'new wine' churches will be often unrecognisable in culture and practise to those who pioneered reformation in the not far gone 70's and 80's. But the transformation will be Heaven's joy as it releases indescribable measures of newfound grace to Earth.

So, here we have a brief compilation of all this writer can see for now; but Oh! How my heart races at the new discoveries that are just around the corner for those who stay faithful and hungry!

BEWARE OF OFFENSE

Might I put in a word of caution? - Transitional Revelatory Keys are very often hidden in the midst of things that offend. Offence has a tendency to on one hand harden and 'lift up' the proud while on the other to cause the heart of the humble to 'stoop low' and further soften . . . . . like the effect of the sun on wax or clay.

Revelation is being poured out to the church of how to better position herself to fulfil her role on the earth. There is so much that The HOLY SPIRIT wants His Bride to attain to, in order that we become that bride without spot or blemish. Here are some of the areas where change is on its way.

FATHER-GOD, JESUS & The HOLY SPIRIT

1. A shift in our grasp, understanding and revelation from 'The LORD' to 'The FATHER, ABBA, PAPA-GOD'. A change in emphasis from what we've been saved from to who we've been saved to become. From saved sinner to redeemed king. An emphasis of the Fatherhood of GOD not only the revelation of Jesus our Saviour.

2. Overcoming a religious stronghold that seeks to make the life and ministry of JESUS the pinnacle of achievement beyond which no believer should aspire to rise. This thought pattern seeks to make His works exclusive whereas His charge to His church was to carry on the very same works! The church must grasp the revelation truth that JESUS walked the Earth as a man! Flesh and blood like us. A man. All He achieved was as a result of His union with The HOLY SPIRIT and The FATHER. GOD's son walked the Earth as a mortal man; we are called to the same level of intimacy and communion with The HOLY SPIRIT and the same love for FATHER GOD. Mature sons and daughters of GOD will again walk the earth doing the exact same works that HE did and more. This will be to JESUS's great joy and fulfilment.

3. A new vitality in our relationship with The HOLY SPIRIT as one who delights to encourage, befriend and 'hang out' with us.

So we 'tarry', we 'soak', we 'abide' and we 'marinate' in His Presence. We find a place of rest in Him free from guilt that questions our sitting at the feet of JESUS - "Ought we not to be interceding for the lost?" our Martha mind asks. This rest comes from a further outworking of the revelation of PAPA's acceptance of us as His sons and daughters - when He looks at you, He is happy, He sees the reflection of Himself in His creation! Wow!

SPIRITUAL GIFTS

4. A renewed emphasis on prophecy as part of our inheritance in The Baptism of The HOLY SPIRIT, a shift from 'Tongues' to 'Prophecy'. From self-edification to the edification of others. A shift from prophetic revelation honing in on the revealing of secret, hidden sin to now revealing and unearthing hidden grace; One brings into shame, the other releases into destiny.

5. A new understanding that prophecy is not just a public, pulpit ministry but a one-on-one personal ministry calling for every saint. We are all empowered to edify one another in love through exercising prophetic graces. "You all may prophesy!" "I wish you were all

prophets" (1Corinthians 14:31, Numbers 11:29) "The LORD is with you" released in unction and depth is one of the most powerful prophesies to have impacted me (prophecy - 'forth-telling' for edification, encouragement and comfort - 1Corinthians 14:3).

6. New diversities of anointings in prophetic ministry. Releasing the unction of The Holy Spirit and the accompanying power of GOD not only with the spoken word but also with artistic creativity in drawings, sculptures, paintings, dance, song and theatre.

HOLINESS, LOVE & WHOLENESS

7. From separation to integration. From 'Come out . . and be separate' to 'Go into all the world' a new emphasis on 'into' the world, its systems and operations. Called to be connected & entwined with the world in such closeness as to make the holiness movement of the earlier part of the last century shudder! Called to become relevant, to be so close as to be unmistakeably 'salt and light'. Called to no longer shun the cinemas, pubs & dance halls and all the arenas of life but to take the '7 mountains' of community influence - Business, Government, Family, Church, Education, Media and Entertainment/Arts.

8. Overcoming a harsh judgemental attitude that is symptomatic of the Pharisaical and 'elder brother' heart (Luke 15:27-30) to now be honouring to all men, saint and sinner alike.

9. A fresh pressing into and enacting the revelation of the timeless truth that honour & integrity release life, blessing & longevity. An understanding that the degree to which we hold to honour is that to which grace and life flow.

10. A shift from a need to punish sin, a fear of what to do with "fallen saints and leaders" to an understanding that the price of sin has been forever paid. The pressing need is on how to restore and clean up messes where they occur. Sin has lost its power.

11. Church hierarchy moving from vertical to flat. The anointed, appointed, set man over the congregation can now drink from the funnel of ministry grace from others. He is no longer out there on his own!

REACHING OUT

10. From 'dry' duty bound evangelism to evangelism from a 'spirit overflow', inebriated with HIS power and touch on our lives; 'These men are (contrary to how they appear to be carrying on) not drunk' Peter hastily offered as an excuse for those fresh

with The SPIRIT's touch. As a consequence of this new filling The Church moves from being on the street corners armed only with microphones & gospel tracts and into prophetic evangelism with new levels of creativity; evangelising no longer just with the '4 spiritual laws' and the Roman Road but armed with the prophetic, revelatory, and power gifts of The HOLY SPIRIT.

11. A motive of evangelising to avoid the guilt of not telling the sinner, 'lest their blood be on my hands' to one of now displaying The FATHER's goodness because HE is a good GOD, and we are overflowing with HIS love! A heart now being armed with a security in HIM and a subsequent overflow of the love & goodness that 'leads men to repentance'.

12. From evangelising to 'just being nice'. From 'going out on evangelism' as a program to living evangelism in a supernaturally natural way.

13. From the goal being church growth to being kingdom growth. From "I want you to be part of my church" to "I just want to bless you and release GOD's goodness to you" (even if I don't tell you what church I go to)

CHURCH LIFE & MISSION

14. The walls & barriers breaking down as 'immigrant churches' shift from being 'ethnic' churches to culturally embracing congregations. Similarly, the middle class no longer remains the majority as the working classes streams into The KINGDOM. A new level of grace for cross-cultural missions is being 'zapped by' The SPIRIT into the DNA of the believer. As class and ethnic insecurities are rapidly overcome a new race will start off to get to every tribe, nation and tongue.

15. A return from 'building centred' to 'home centred' meetings as new levels of 'koinonia' and newfound freedom to share communal love and intimacy are discovered by The Church. Hospitality, which is a foundation of the gifts, (1Peter 4:9, Romans 12:13 etc) operates at its zenith in our homes. The home no longer a 'castle' but a 'vestibule' as The FATHER heart of GOD is seen and released through The Body.

5-FOLD MINISTRY

16. The emphasis no longer being on the operation and flow of 5-fold ministries as the height of Christian service. Equipping the saints for the work of the ministry now taking precedence, all being called to do the

work of the ministry. From leaders doing it all by themselves to equipping the church with their DNA to also function in the same graces.

17. A continued releasing of the saints into 5 - fold equipping ministries in 'the world' and the market place. 'Kings' and 'Priests' being sent by the church into the world systems in much the same way as Paul & Silas were commissioned to the Gentile nations.

18. A shift from pastoral ministry based 'in house' to being based 'in city'. With it a new release of grace before local councils and government. This leading to an emerging abundance of new partnerships between local councils and churches.

19. The releasing and recognition of prophets and apostles in certain parts of the world in the 90's & 00's culminating in a shifting from 'Pastor-Administrator' led, to 'Apostle-Prophet' led, church government.

20. A theological shift from the admin-pastor-teacher perspective on doctrine to the 'can do' apostle-prophet approach. What a great difference between the likely exposition of John 14:12 from a teacher-pastor and a prophet-apostle. The offices are designed to work differently for a purpose.

21. Change from an emphasis on titles and office to sonship. A new level of security in our identity in Christ, the validity of our inheritance to walk as sons. Complete and entire without a need for titles.

22. The emphasis for growing believers anxious to fulfil their calling no longer just on, "What 5 fold ministry am I called to?" but which of the '7 mountains' of community influence - Business, Government, Family, Church, Education, Media and Entertainment/Arts am I called to?"

23. We enter a time where leaders are not just measured by the size of their ministries numerically as much as by the degree of kingdom influence they exert in society.

PRAYER & REVIVAL

24. Prayer from the view of the Earth to from a view from the Heavens. The former being based on what we see in the natural realm, the other being based on perspectives from heaven as viewed in the spiritual realm. So we learn to pray as kings seated in heavenly places as we bring down and release more of The Kingdom rather than releasing the cries of servants and paupers (who are on the earth) from earth up to heaven.

25. Change from a 'shot-in-the-arm' view of revival - 'so as to sustain us', 'to bring life back into the church' so 'The Church doesn't shrivel up and die', to a hunger for and embracing of a continuous revival lifestyle leading to outbreaks and outpourings.

HEALING, ANGELS AND MIRACLES

26. From Word based churches to Power <u>and</u> Word based churches. Paul spoke of the kingdom of GOD being established in demonstrations of The SPIRIT and of Power not (only in) words. (1Corinthians 2:4,5 & 4:20) A sense of security in being 'word based' without an accompanying hunger for demonstrations of power is negligent. It leads to spiritual coldness. Where there is no hunger, lukewarmness settles in. "All word no spirit will dry up, all spirit and no word will blow up, spirit plus word will grow up!"

27. A shift in belief systems about healing stemming from a new grasp of the kindness & generosity of FATHER GOD. Healing no longer being (perceived as) a lottery of 'only if GOD wills to', to 'GOD is in a good mood today and everyday', YES! HE is willing!

28. In the ministering of healing a move from the standpoint of "take it by faith brother!"

to "on a scale of one to ten, how is your pain now?". Now able to ask the question, "When we prayed for you what did you feel?" without negating faith.

29. A new willingness and freedom from fear to embrace an awareness of the role of angels in helping us in countless ways. From Elijah asking for his servants' eyes to be opened to Peter being rescued from jail these encounters are there as our inheritance, how could we have missed this for so long?

PRAISE & WORSHIP

30. From Praise and Worship to Praise / Worship and Intimacy and SPIRIT break out.

ESCHATOLOGY

31. A shift in eschatological perspective from 'If The LORD tarries', 'Get me out of here!' syndrome to a new heart cry for 'The kingdoms of this world have become the kingdoms of our GOD'. No longer trapped in a mindset of "JESUS may come tomorrow so what is the purpose of planning?"

32. An emphasis on focusing on the coming generations, investing in the youth as ones who will "walk on our ceilings as their floors".

31

New Wine

CHAPTER 2
A revelation of
PAPA-GOD, HOLY
SPIRIT and THE LORD
JESUS

"May the grace of the Lord Jesus
Christ, and the love of God, and
the fellowship of the Holy Spirit
be with you all"
2Corinthians 13:14

We are called to deepen our understanding of and relationship with GOD The FATHER, The Son & The HOLY SPIRIT.

Traditionally we have often referred to 'The LORD' in our speaking and praying patterns. This is good but we are called to deepen our grasp of who The FATHER is and who The HOLY SPIRIT is. Both promise to be exciting revelations and discoveries for us.

PAPA-GOD

Let's begin with The FATHER. 'Father' means various things to us among which are love, safety, security, provision and discipline.

I want to say, FATHER loves you very dearly, you are unique and extremely special to Him. He adores you, literally. Yes He adores you! Our FATHER works in our lives like an earthly father would to teach and train us as sons and daughters; to bring us up into maturity. Where and when necessary to apply a level of discipline to make us align with who we are called to be as sons.

Called to walk as mature heirs

I use the word 'sons' (as a gender inclusive term) as opposed to children as it carries a connotation of maturity and dependability. To walk as heirs we need to be trained and disciplined. 'The rod and rebuke bring wisdom but a child left to himself brings shame[8]'. As it is in the natural realm so it is in the spiritual realm. How does our heavenly FATHER train and discipline us? In our spirits, in that part of us that hears his voice and receives his rebuke. Oh such pain and grieving in our spirits when he tells us off for being immature or childish or disobedient! Such grief in our hearts when He chastises us.

Rebukes for sin

There is little need for anything other means to 'tell us off' when He can 'tell us off' deep down in our hearts. I remember a few times when He used the rod on my heart . . . . the threat of His voice, of a loss of peace in my heart, 'Oh LORD forgive me!' I would cry, 'I'm sorry LORD, take away Your rebuke and restore joy and gladness to my heart and soul!' would be my plea.

Tests of obedience

If The FATHER is going to use you He will test, try and prove you in the furnace of obedience. I recall a time I was told by FATHER to go to America for a period of time. I did not know for how long I was going to be away. Around the 23rd day of what was to initially be a four-day stay my patience wore thin and I went to rebel in my heart. I will never forget the warning of The HOLY SPIRIT – He spoke such a clear and immediate word of warning

---

[8] Proverbs 29:15

to me, 'Rebellion!' it was like a mum would yell to her 5 year old about to cross the road into oncoming traffic. Immediately I rescinded and sought for grace to stay in obedience to my FATHER; as I did so grace came to see Hebrews 12: 1-16 in a new light. My receiving chastisement from The FATHER was a measure of His love and purposes for my life.

Our provider and safety net

The other thing that we are called to learn as we progress to become mature sons is utter reliance on DADDY in heaven to keep us safe whatever comes our way. To do this He may allow us to be placed in situations where our 'faith muscle' is tested. He wants us to learn to obey when He instructs, to have faith to move when He says 'move', to stand when He says 'stand still'. If you want to be a man of GOD then there is a SWOT team-training regimen for you! The wonderful thing is as you humble yourself and lean on His grace, grace will flow your way. If ever you are so silly as to allow pride and independence, 'after all it is voluntary service' you say, the tap of grace will be severely restricted and you will be in deep water without the sustenance of grace. So in times of testing, stay humble, leave pride outside the door and you will do just fine as you learn to lean on the grace and mercy of FATHER GOD (Hebrews 4:16)

We see this in the life of Moses brother, Aaron. Due to a transgression on their part, two of Aaron's sons

were killed by fire from the FATHER instantly. Do you know that Aaron was not allowed to bury them? Rather Moses called for others to carry them out to be buried. Not only this, later on Aaron and his other surviving sons were rebuked by Moses for failing to carry out their functions properly after this! This is the height of discipline in their service to The FATHER. Are we called to such levels of fortitude? Let us strive to be the best we can, vessels of honour to our GOD. In times of hardship and distress let us learn to salute and say, 'Yes Sir' as we still carry out our service to The KINGDOM with honour and dignity. Amen.

'Endure hardship as good soldiers of JESUS CHRIST[9]', Paul wrote to his spiritual son, Timothy. There is a bonding that only comes between son and dad when dad has raised and where appropriate meted our correctional discipline. If you want to know your FATHER in heaven more ask Him to chastise you in love and mercy.

It will do wonders for your character. We get to share in His character when we are raised in The FATHER'S love as well as His discipline. 'Woe to you O land when your princes are children' If you

---

[9] 2Timothy 2:3

aspire to be entrusted to rule and reign, ask for grace to recognise and receive discipline.

Build from your love for The LORD to a strong foundation of revelation knowledge of GOD as your PAPA-GOD.

THE HOLY SPIRIT

The other area of transition in our experiential knowledge is our walk with HOLY SPIRIT. Wow! Now this is the most dynamic of our relationships; this is meant to be so. He is the One sent to the earth to teach us, to comfort us, to walk with us. But I must warn you treasure and guard this relationship FAR ABOVE all others. A wrong heart, a wrong turn, a bad decision and He will withdraw from you. He will leave you so quietly and gently that you will scarcely even know that He has left the room! 'O teach me to guard my heart HOLY SPIRIT'. What do I mean by this? That you will lose your salvation? No. That GOD will know longer be with you? No. But the sweet communion will no longer be there. The romance and sparkle of your friendship can quickly dissipate if care is not taken.

Just like a husband pays attention to the likes and dislikes of his wife, so we learn how to woo The Presence of HOLY SPIRIT. We learn to sing to The HOLY SPIRIT, to walk ever so gently so as not to lose that aroma of Heaven on our lives. We learn the things that HOLY SPIRIT likes and approves of as well as what irks or irritates HIM. In our 'spirit-walk' we learn to tread gently, to walk circumspectly, to talk softly and wisely.

A new vitality comes to our relationship with The HOLY SPIRIT as one who delights to comfort and encourage us as we 'tarry', 'soak', 'abide' or 'marinate' in HIS Presence. Not striving in prayers for something as often done in the past but resting in Him. This being a further outworking of the revelation of PAPA's acceptance of us as His sons and daughters – when He looks at you, He sees Himself in there!

In the new move of GOD our lives are built on the foundation of our revelation and relationships with The FATHER, The SON and The HOLY SPIRIT.

'IDENTITY plus INTIMACY leads to new IMPACT & EFFECTIVENESS'

This new revelation in our understanding of The FATHER and The SON opens up new realms of discovery in who we are called to be as well as how we are called to minister. As a ministry colleague puts it, 'Identity and Intimacy leads to Impact'. Our identity comes from our relationship with The FATHER. When coupled with a new level of intimacy with HOLY SPIRIT our impact increases in the world around us.

A revelation solely of JESUS as our saviour leaves one grateful as redeemed from death and sin but can leave us relatively lame, powerless and inactive.

Our deepened revelation and practical outworking of a relationship with The FATHER prepares us for battle, for life and for preparing to take charge of FATHER'S business. As in the natural we bear our father's name so in the spiritual we take on our place in the family business as we spend time getting acquainted with PAPA-GOD.

Our intimacy with The HOLY SPIRIT removes the frustration and pressure of 'trying to be a good Christian', 'trying to do the right thing'. He is the One who empowers us and leads us in service. It is as we spend time in communing with Him that our lives are touched, strengthened and renewed. In the process we are empowered for service - effortlessly. The exertion that is required is to keep in touch, in communion. He looks after the rest.

Revelation of Papa GOD

CHAPTER 3
Worship & GOD'S Presence

"All the Levites who were musicians--Asaph, Heman, Jeduthun and their sons and relatives-- stood on the east side of the altar, dressed in fine linen and playing cymbals, harps and lyres. They were accompanied by 120 priests sounding trumpets. 13 The trumpeters and singers joined in unison, as with one voice, to give praise and thanks to the LORD. Accompanied by trumpets, cymbals and other instruments, they raised their voices in praise to the LORD and sang: "He is good; his love endures forever." Then the temple of the LORD was filled with a cloud, 14 and the priests could not perform their service because of the cloud, for the glory of the LORD filled the temple of God" 2Chronicles 5:12-14

PROPHETIC WORD

The worship of the people must change. There must be more of The FATHER in the meetings and less of our preaching. We must learn to tarry and wait in His Presence. We must learn to tarry and not move until His cloud rests on us. We must develop meetings where there is no preaching of the word, we only come to sit at His feet and wait before Him. Meetings where we stand back and allow Him to minister to the people. Moses tarried before the LORD for forty days, completely overwhelmed by The GLORY of GOD, His manifest glory.

The Glory Cloud coming down and resting on the top of the mountain will be a manifestation of the new move of GOD where His Presence and Glory will come to rest on entire towns and cities for days a time. It will just sit and wait on a region until all that FATHER desires to accomplish there has been accomplished. It will just tarry and wait. Sitting as it were at the entrance to certain towns waiting for the response of the elders at the gate.

The power of GOD will flow and healing miracles of all types and kinds will manifest in those days says The LORD. My power will sweep through and destroy works of evil and darkness in the twinkling of an eye. Much responsibility will rest on my church to rebuild neighbourhoods and corral the harvests in says the LORD. It must be done skilfully, quickly says The LORD that no place be found for the enemy says The LORD. My word and My teachings must be introduced like to a virgin territory. Teams will sweep in and build My Kingdom in the hearts of those who have been swept in by My Glory. So many testimonies to record for posterity. Wow!

MANIFESTATIONS OF GOD'S SPECIAL PRESENCE

In the last half of April each year over the years 2008 to 2010 as I sought for the new move of GOD I was blessed with a special experience. These occurred on Saturday April 26th 2008 in Lakeland, Florida; Wednesday April 22nd 2009 in Ibadan, Nigeria and Sunday April 25th 2010 in Whitstable, Kent.

The experience was the grace of GOD through the spiritual impartation and gift of 'discerning of spirits' on me to perceive a manifestation of The Cloud of GOD's Glory. Accompanying this was a marked level of The Presence of The HOLY SPIRIT in a meeting. I believe that the degree of receptivity and preparation of the leaders and people in each occasion affected the longevity or otherwise of this tangible sense of GOD's Presence.

To seek to explain this phenomenon, which I feel, will be part of the last day's church let us look at a time in Israel's history when they experienced this in Exodus 33

"Then the LORD said to Moses, "Depart and go up from here, you and the people whom you have brought out of the land of Egypt, to the land of which I swore to Abraham, Isaac, and Jacob, saying, 'To your descendants I will give it.' And I will send My Angel before you, and I will drive out the Canaanite and the Amorite and the Hittite and the Perizzite and the Hivite and the Jebusite"

- Moses is given an instruction and promised an angel for his help. .

"Go up to a land flowing with milk and honey; for I will not go up in your midst, lest I consume you on the way, for you are a stiff-necked people."

- The reason for this is that The LORD's manifest Presence must be handled and accommodated sensitively & respectfully. It is as if GOD is not sure at this time that His people have this degree of sensitivity.

"And when the people heard this bad news, they mourned, and no one put on his ornaments. For the LORD had said to Moses, "Say to the children of Israel, 'You are a stiff-necked people. I could come up into your midst in one moment and consume you. Now therefore, take off your ornaments, that I may know what to do to you.'" So the children of

Israel stripped themselves of their ornaments by Mount Horeb"

- The people mourned on hearing this and The LORD called for 'time out' to see what other courses of action may be available . . .

"Moses took his tent and pitched it outside the camp, far from the camp, and called it the tabernacle of meeting. And it came to pass that everyone who sought the LORD went out to the tabernacle of meeting which was outside the camp. So it was, whenever Moses went out to the tabernacle, that all the people rose, and each man stood at his tent door and watched Moses until he had gone into the tabernacle. And it came to pass, when Moses entered the tabernacle, that the pillar of cloud descended and stood at the door of the tabernacle, and the LORD talked with Moses. All the people saw the pillar of cloud standing at the tabernacle door, and all the people rose and worshiped, each man in his tent door. So the LORD spoke to Moses face to face, as a man speaks to his friend. And he would return to the camp, but his servant Joshua the son of Nun, a young man, did not depart from the tabernacle"

- Moses and Joshua however were familiar with The Presence of GOD, they lived off it, they understood it, and they knew the

protocols & etiquette of how to behave when
in the manifest Presence of The KING.

"Then Moses said to the LORD, "See, You say to
me, 'Bring up this people.' But You have not let me
know whom You will send with me. Yet You have
said, 'I know you by name, and you have also
found grace in My sight.' Now therefore, I pray, if I
have found grace in Your sight, show me now Your
way, that I may know You and that I may find
grace in Your sight. And consider that this nation is
Your people."

"And He said, "My Presence will go with you, and
I will give you rest." Then he said to Him, "If Your
Presence does not go with us, do not bring us up
from here. For how then will it be known that Your
people and I have found grace in Your sight, except
You go with us? So we shall be separate, Your
people and I, from all the people who are upon the
face of the earth." So the LORD said to Moses, "I
will also do this thing that you have spoken; for
you have found grace in My sight, and I know you
by name."

- Subsequently the prospect of life in
  leadership without the assurance of the
  promise of GOD's continued manifest (felt,
  perceived, tangible & palpable) Presence
  was totally untenable! 'Without Your
  Presence LORD we're going nowhere, we'll
  just stop this whole mission' was their cry.

48

"And he said, "Please, show me Your glory. Then He said, "I will make all My goodness pass before you, and I will proclaim the name of the LORD before you. I will be gracious to whom I will be gracious, and I will have compassion on whom I will have compassion." But He said, "You cannot see My face; for no man shall see Me, and live." And the LORD said, "Here is a place by Me, and you shall stand on the rock. So it shall be, while My glory passes by, that I will put you in the cleft of the rock, and will cover you with My hand while I pass by. Then I will take away My hand, and you shall see My back; but My face shall not be seen."

- As leaders they knew that with His Presence the glory of GOD would also be revealed, in changed lives, in miracles, in supernatural supply, it all would flow from His Glory revealed as GOD chose to tabernacle daily with His people . . .

THE ISSUE

So what needs to so desperately change? I suggest the issue is that so few of us as leaders are comfortable with the high levels of GOD's Presence that occur when FATHER turns up the notch on The SPIRIT's Presence - by even a few degrees! So to cover for this we commonly end up letting out some awkward gaff like Peter did on the mount of transfiguration or we become hyper-nervous that someone may prophecy, or that someone will start speaking in a supernatural language. Immediately we begin to dust off and rehearse our favourite

(doctrinal) tools and means of SPIRIT (crowd?) control. When it's all over we breathe a sigh of relief that the atmosphere has returned to normal, We can breathe now and proceed with our (well thought out and structured) meeting. 'Whew! That was a close one', we sigh inwardly as we glance furtively at the faces of our elders to make sure no one was offended by that display of uncontrolled 'emotional excess' or by doing anything at odds with our present level of spiritual understanding.

We are happy for a bit of The Presence of GOD, but not too much! It makes our people feel uncomfortable. And the visitors? Well we would not want them to offended - by GOD (too strongly) breaking into our meetings would we?

Does this strike a bell somewhere? Yet what is REVIVAL if it is not GOD breaking into our gatherings, our communities and our nations?

NOT A LICENSE FOR LACK OF LEADERSHIP

Now hear me, I am not prescribing meetings of uncontrolled excess with no one assuming accountability and taking leadership and guiding the people along to drink of the waters of The

SPIRIT. These being poured out in an atmosphere of Heaven released on HIS sons and daughters.

But what I am saying is that so few of us are equipped to be conductors of The FATHER's manifest Presence. When His presence comes we hide, we run away, we struggle just as Adam and Eve did after the fall. Yet surely one of our primary functions as leaders ought to be to bring people into The Presence of our loving FATHER?

There is only one way to learn to do this - in the confines of times of personal intimacy and devotion to The LORD when He visits us one to one. We as leaders are shown up in public when an unusual sense of The SPIRIT's Presence descends on a meeting and we do not know what to do, what to say or how to proceed and bungle things. It is simply a reflection of the fact we are not habitually experiencing this realm of intimacy with The LORD in private.

HANDLING THE GLORY OF GOD WHEN IT COMES

Three key points I believe invaluable in rightly receiving and 'stewarding' The Presence of GOD: -

A. Our acquired skill

- Yes, great skill is needed in handling the Presence of GOD. But we can learn this!

- How to ensure the channels and the atmosphere are kept open to receive more of it.
- How to manage & transmit The Presence when it does come.

To 'manage' I refer to having an (almost innate) ability to receive it (like a lightning pole receives power) and then feed that Presence, Power and Anointing into growing the atmosphere of Heaven in a meeting. It is my humble impression that few of us as leaders know what to do when HIS Presence comes in a deep and powerful way. Now I firmly believe that this quality will either spawn increase on a move of GOD or kill it. If we as leaders are not schooled in handling The FATHER's Presence our scope for containing a supernatural move of GOD will be seriously limited. It is a vital key - How to receive, build upon and appropriately handle, steward and integrate The Presence of GOD in a meeting.

B. Guiding the people

An <u>overly</u> open microphone policy will not work. Too open a microphone policy can result in dampening the flow of The Spirit in a meeting; it only takes one immature or emotional or 'attention seeking' or simply 'out of time' contributor to cause a 'prophetic mush', where the meeting goes nowhere in terms of an intended prophetic flow.

This does not mean that everyone is not welcome to approach the front to offer a word but as leaders WE must lovingly and discerningly know when what someone is offering is stifling and reducing the atmosphere! The aim of the game is for everyone who contributes to leave the microphone (platform) hotter then they met it, with the dial of Presence of GOD going up not down!

So first place is see those who wish to speak with the eye of your heart, are they the ones to share, sing, pray or prophecy next? If they start and you see it wasn't for now, then with love, a smile, a big hug a prayer and an assurance to hear more of what they want to share later wean them off the microphone and quickly get back on track (When this happens experience tells us we only have a few seconds to move - so act!) Signal to the worship team to bring back in place the atmosphere of heaven as you wait on GOD again . . stay hungry, stay open, stay willing. If you must look at your watch to see where things, are do it most gently and carefully, how would you feel if you were out on your first date and your partner looked at their watch? (Yes - even our attitudes shown in our actions grieve The SPIRIT of GOD). Be bold and brave in asking the people to do something to cause FATHER's Presence to break in. Once I saw a worship leader (sensitively) ask everyone to kneel and heaven invaded us.

C. Recognising those with grace in an area different from ours

Sometimes when working as a team it's great to recognise whom in the leadership is most prophetically inclined and thus best equipped to lead when you discern an unusual sense of GOD in the building. Hand over as soon as you can.

Back in Nigeria when I was part of a team of five leading a regular daily meeting of from 50 to 400 people I recall there being such trust and liberty between us all that I once interrupted a fellow leaders sermon as I saw GOD begin to break in and sensed our needing to take the meeting in a different direction. Obviously this was rare but the team worked well enough for us to be comfortable to practise this. We would obviously appraise events afterwards. Interestingly this period of prayer and an openness and availability to the prophetic moves of GOD over the period 1996-98 has resulted in a church planting movement birthing over 100 churches in over 15 nations to date. Amazing what GOD can do when we cooperate with His HOLY SPIRIT!

WORSHIP - an invitation

I write this with a sense that Papa-GOD longs to invade our meetings with His strong, sweet presence. FATHER longs for our worship to not just be a (demeaning) ritual of, 'We'll sing a song as we take up the offering' or 'Shall we rise to sing

before we invite our guest speaker to the platform'. GOD Almighty longs for our worship to be an invitation to Him by His people to come and meet with them, that in doing so we and all who are with us may encounter Him and through that encounter receive life, be transformed into the image of His Son and be empowered to reflect the same Glory. But how far as leaders are we prepared to go with this? Are we content in the shallow waters of, 'Thank you pastor, that was a nice service' or are we willing to take the risk of 'Wow! I'm totally changed! / My life can never be the same again! / Can you carry me out of here?'

PROPHETIC PROMISE OF FRESH RAIN

Yea, I do see a fresh wave of passion & zeal coming on the church, some will try to control it and will find themselves swept away . . .

"For I will move in My power and My deluge of fresh rain will come on this generation says Your GOD. Move out of the way, move your plans and your ordinances, your statutes, for My SPIRIT will come among you and give you fresh ways, fresh understanding that will be key to the move of My Power to sweep through all the nations of the earth. So humble yourselves before Me and your doctrines before Me for there is yet much that this generation has not been able to grasp, for Me to reveal from Heaven. Yet it is locked up in My Word which you read daily but with no insight to these things says the LORD. So seek me, seek me for the rain as my word says (Zechariah 10:1), for there is a new rain of My Power and glory coming

that the world has never before seen since the days of my apostles and prophets yet is even now being restored says The Lord, and I will confound those who say they are experts and theologians for I will bring to pass a new thing in your day says The LORD - so seek me earnestly says The LORD, seek Me and you will never seek Me in vain for I desire to pour out My SPIRIT on this part of the world without measure as I said (Joel 2:28), fear not you who have waited and been tireless in seeking Me, it will come to pass shortly. Stay at your posts, I am The LORD."

So, do we feel that we will be entrusted with manifestations of FATHER's Glory Presence? The cry of my heart is to see His Presence come again, yes . . but even more for it to come and REST on a people to accomplish and finish a work that will not end until we see Him coming in the clouds . . . may such communities of believers be found who are led by those who by their humility and surrender, sacrifice and consecration, hunger and faithfulness will keep aspiring until like Enoch 'their place is no longer found[10]'. Amen.

---

[10] Genesis 5:24

Building on 'PRAISE & WORSHIP'

In charismatic circles it is sometimes almost as if we have a formula for our worship time. A slow song to start with, then a few fast praise songs, then back into some slow songs of worship. As we get towards the end of the time allotted to worship the pastor steps forwards to take the microphone and move into the next stage of the meeting. For the non-charismatic meeting it is as songs are interspersed in the meeting in order to add variety. How can we adjust to align more with what heaven wants?

1. Our worship needs to be seen as an invitation to GOD to come and tabernacle with His people. An invite to stay and rest on His children. So the aim of the worship (and those who lead it) must be to bring the people into FATHER's presence.

2. Having ushered the people into The FATHER's Presence the next thing is to wait to allow FATHER to now touch and minister to His people. NOT rush in to our message or the announcements!

3. Often the way that FATHER will touch and bless His people will be through the prophetic gifting in the church leadership. He will seek to use those whose spiritual eyes and senses are more attuned that others

57

to know what is going on the realm of the spirit as GOD pours out his love and affection on His children. As leaders we need to recognise and give room for the sensitive ones in our leadership to present what GOD has on offer at the moment. It could be a word of healing, of encouragement, of reconciliation, the list is endless.

4. So as to usher GOD's people into this realm of divine atmosphere we need to add another level of music and singing to our worship slot – INTIMACY. Intimacy and new songs.

INTIMACY & NEW SONGS

Intimacy is when we are singing songs to The FATHER at a level that is deeper than our exuberant praise and worship. How do we describe intimacy in our worship? That which is offered barely above a whisper, something that oozes from the heart of a lover, an offering that is unique and personal. This often works best coming from just one source with very selective musical accompaniment. It gently ushers in The PRESENCE of The King in a deep, powerful and special way. Sometimes old and familiar songs struggle to carry the outflow from our hearts to our King. We long to be able to express the deeper yearnings of our heart in worship. We reach deep down inside our hearts looking for a new release of our love and gratitude to GOD. And as we look deep down, The

SPIRIT helps our spirits to bring out something new that we've never sung before – a new song[11]! A new expression of our love. And Oh how beautiful is the sound! This new sound pierces the heavens and causes heaven to come down! It ushers in that which is new, that which heaven desires to birth on the earth, a new move of The SPIRIT of GOD in the hearts of men. It is not just 'a new song'! it releases the heart of GOD in response to the heart cry of man. In every new move of GOD, in every place where revival is breaking out there will be signature tunes, melodies that mark, release and characterise the heart of what GOD is doing on the earth. New songs and new moves go hand in hand with each other.

For this reason I am always encouraging churches to reach for new songs, new melodies, new tunes that describe and bear witness to what GOD is doing on the earth. Granted once in while it can be a blessing to look back in time and reach from a melody that was once new on earth. But this ought to always be the exception rather than the rule.

DANCE & BANNERS

It is as we express ourselves, as we give release to what is going on in our hearts that creative and

---

[11] Psalm 40:3, 96:1, 98:1 etc

prophetic praise and worship are released. Our spirits yearn to release more of ourselves to GOD in thanks and adoration. The HOLY SPIRIT comes alongside us to empower us to release us in this way.

Two additional ways we are seeing this is in the dance and with banners and flags. Some mindsets

seem to think that this is for children to do. Well, yes it is something that children can do, but it is also a powerful expression of praise from the mature warrior! As a great leader puts it, 'It is freeing', yes of ourselves and also of heaven!

CHAPTER 4
From Tongues to Prophecy

"And afterward, I will pour out my Spirit on all
people. Your sons and daughters will prophesy,
your old men will dream dreams; your young men
will see visions. Even on my servants, both men
and women, I will pour out my Spirit in those
days"
Joel 2:28,29

A new emphasis is coming on prophecy as part of our inheritance in The Baptism of The HOLY SPIRIT. This will produce a shift from 'Tongues' to 'Prophecy'; from self-edification to the edification of others.

The charismatic movement has had a focus on the baptism of the HOLY SPIRIT 'with the initial evidence of speaking in tongues'. This movement brought in a whole new generation of believers empowered by The HOLY SPIRIT depending on what stream we have come from. We can think of figures ranging from David du Plessis aka 'Mr Pentecost' to Demos Shakarian who founded the Full Gospel Businessmen's Fellowship.

The emphasis was on the baptism of the HOLY SPIRIT as a second experience after ones conversion. The 'proof' of one being baptised in the spirit was the ability to speak in tongues. We have seen a generation of believers come to faith and grow as believers with this emphasis in their practical Christian life.

Speaking in tongues has numerous benefits and blessings, some writers speak of as many as 50 reasons why to speak in tongues – this is great. I for one speak in tongues for hours at a time. But I'd like us to look a little beyond speaking in tongues. Interestingly when Peter stood up to defend what was going on outside the upper room on the day of

Pentecost he chose a passage from the OT[12] which spoke of visions, dreams and prophecy but omitted tongues as a manifestation of being filled by The SPIRIT.

Let's ask ourselves what Paul had to say about building on the necessary foundation of speaking in tongues? Mainly two things, one was that we are to ask for the power to interpret our tongues. The others is that we are to also covet to prophesy.

Now in charismatic circles both of these have been practised from time to time, true; But for the most part by a select special few and almost exclusively from the podium. In the move we are entering into however the whole church is being graced to speak in tongues, interpret tongues as well as prophesy. These elementary gifts will operate as a foundation and platform for the other spiritual gifts. This is where The LORD wants us to set our gaze – the higher gifts!

It is interesting that it was on Paul's 3rd missionary journey several years after the day of Pentecost that when he prayed for people to receive The HOLY SPIRIT they received both gifts at the same time! (Acts 19:6). Prior to this we only hear of speaking in tongues accompanying the in- filling of The SPIRIT.

Looking at 1Corinthians 14 we see that The LORD desired for a community of believers where there

---

[12] Joel 2:28,29

are not only gatherings where all pray in tongues but also meetings where all prophesy! Stay with me as I make a distinction here between forms of prophecy. We will also clarify Paul's words about only allowing for two or three prophesies in a meeting at a time. But first let us make a distinction regarding praying in tongues aka praying in the spirit and proclaiming 'a tongue'.

In the most often used form of speaking in tongues we are praying to GOD in a language that is a mystery to all but GOD. This is often referred to as 'praying in the spirit'. This form of prayer by its very definition needs no interpretation; you are speaking mysteries to GOD. In another form of praying however, the direction of discourse has changed from us to GOD to from GOD to us. This form when accompanied by an interpretation is the equivalent of a prophecy (1Corinthians 14:5) This latter form of praying in tongues requires a grace that is different from praying in the spirit. It also releases a greater anointing, as it is GOD who now desires to speak to HIS people. We are enjoined to ask for the gift to subsequently interpret tongues.
When both work together this is equivalent to a prophetic word. I have been blessed when not knowing what to do a tongue and interpretation have been released. May I also add that it is even more beautiful when the person who gives the tongue leaves the interpretation of tongue to another to complete.

Ok, back to forms of prophesying. The simple gift of prophesying is to encourage and uplift people. It does not have to include any special revelation to be a genuine word from The FATHER that blesses, encourages and uplifts.

In the instance of a prophecy being accompanied by specific knowledge about a person's past, present or future choices as revealed by a word of knowledge and word of wisdom respectively it can amount to a 'directive word' from The LORD, which brings a new set of protocols into place. Typically a third person who is in authority may then need to validate, test or 'judge' the word. This is with a view to protect the speaker as well as the recipient.

A simple word of prophesy only carries a function of lifting a persons sprits up and very often quotes a simple biblical truth or principle. Take for example, 'The LORD is with you' as a word does not necessarily require judging in the same way. It is this simple form of prophesying that I refer to as one that all of a community of believers can be involved in at the same time.

How?

Firstly, by one of several means and methods: - For example by sharing words about biblical characters that may apply to a person, by looking at what they are wearing and trusting GOD to use this to give you a word for them or by finding the first word that comes to your head and speaking it in faith as you trust GOD for more.

Secondly this can be done in pairs or in small groups gathered in a circle. This way everyone can go home uplifted by a prophetic word!

The emphasis in prophecy ought not to be to reveal the sins of people as much as to reveal the redemptive gifting and good in people! So there is coming a shift from prophetic revelation honing in on the revealing of secret, hidden sin to now revealing and unearthing hidden grace; One brings into shame, the other releases into destiny.

A new understanding has now come that prophecy is not as much a public, pulpit ministry as a one-on-one personal ministry and calling for every saint. All empowered to edify one another in love through exercising prophetic graces. "You all may prophesy![13]"

A new grace is being released to transition from just speaking out prophecies to a myriad of release mechanisms. There is a new diversity of anointings in prophetic ministry: - Releasing the unction of The Holy Spirit not only with the spoken word but also with artistic creativity in drawings, paintings, dance, song and theatre.

---

[13] 1Corinthians 14:31

CHAPTER 5
APOSTLES
Who on Earth needs them? Who are they & what do they do? Do we (still) need them?

"Now, therefore, you are no longer strangers and foreigners, but fellow citizens with the saints and members of the household of God, having been built on the foundation of the apostles and prophets, Jesus Christ Himself being the chief cornerstone, in whom the whole building, being fitted together, grows into a holy temple in the Lord" Ephesians 2:19-21

I n looking at the task of winning our world to JESUS, we can't but look at how Paul and his teams were equipped in the 1st century and desire the same level of equipping today. Part of this search gives rise to the question, 'Are apostles and prophets still needed or valid today?'

This quest for whether apostles and prophets are still appropriate in the Body of Christ is not because they are to be esteemed higher than the other gifts in a worldly hierarchical sense. Paul makes this clear in Romans[14] - all the parts of The Body are crucial and to be honoured. Administrators, Teachers, Musicians, Deacons, Caretakers, Youth Workers, all valued, all honoured, all very special, all[15]. Rather the quest is simply because they are apparently largely missing! Or, could we more safely put it that, they are very hard to recognise? The very terms 'apostle' and 'prophet' are too often, widely ambiguous and subject to different interpretation. Subsequently even when people do wear these labels they would be more likely shunned than be given room or space to function. (The point of whether they ought to take these titles to themselves like the title 'pastor' was taken in the charismatic era is another debate entirely)

Well, 'Can't we just go on without them?' we ask.

---

[14] Romans 12:4
[15] 1Corinthians 12:12-26

Problem is, how responsible would we be to continue to function with two fifths of Christ's gift and expression of Himself to the church missing? Five key equipping gifts are mentioned[16] in Paul's writings with scores of other ministry gifts dotted around the scriptures[17]. One of the things that make these five significant is that in the descriptions of when JESUS walked the Earth, the gospel and epistle writers refer to Him functioning in all five; An apostle[18], a prophet[19], a teacher, an evangelist and shepherd (pastor). These gifts are the very gifts of Himself and His ability given to us. Given to equip us to successfully build His Church, a process, which He said, the very gates of hell will not be able to withstand!

Now, for us in the 21st century can we imagine attempting to build a car where parts are left out simply because we don't know what those parts do or because they look different from wheels and engines!! It would carry a health warning in bold red writing - "Beware: MISSING PARTS!"

RESTORED GIFTS

Let's look at it this way, over the last sixty odd years we've recognised and accepted at least three of the major ministry gifts. We understand the

---

[16] Ephesians 4:11-13
[17] Romans 12:6-8; 1Corinthians 12:28,29; 1Peter 4:10-11; 1Corinthians 7:7; Ephesians 3:8 etc
[18] Hebrews 3:1
[19] John 4:19

principle that when we receive a gift, we get blessed by what the gift offers; like JESUS said, receive people in their given and proper function and (be entitled to) receive the accompanying reward[20] - the blessings of the grace they walk in!

Evangelists 1950's –

Starting with the evangelist we've seen men like Billy Graham (50's) and Reinhard Bonnke (70's) unravel what it means to us to function in this special grace. A grace where the primary concern is for people to get saved. How the world has been so touched by this ministry! Their focus is on the lost, with a huge passion is for souls, more souls! 'Evangelism, our supreme task' is their battle cry.

Pastors 1960's - (OT equivalent - The Priest)

Then we've seen in the house church / charismatic movement how certain people have this calling to be a pastor and as a result of which thousands have been released to look after thousands of new congregations that this gift has brought to birth. This, as in the progression of all the 5-fold ministry gifts has occurred worldwide; in China, Latin America, North America, Australia and across

Africa. Where would we be without pastors to care for us and nurture us, to dedicate us, marry us

---

[20] Matthew 10:41

and bury us! They focus on the believer. More care, more love, more concern, clucking about like a mother hen, fighting off suspicious looking (potential) sheep stealers!

Teachers 1970's - (OT equivalent - The Scribe)

In between our Sunday services we've learnt to tune into the radio to listen to wonderful Bible messages from teachers like Derek Prince and Joyce Meyer, read books by Watchman Nee and Oswald Chambers and faithfully fed on devotionals by Bob Gass. How richly they have added meaning to so many aspects of our walk with Christ. Without them we'd have fallen so short of all there is for us in Christ! They focus on The Bible.

The 'other gifts'

Now, it ought to go without saying that if many of us have been in the faith long enough to see three "ascension" gifts of Christ restored in our life time (close for this writer!), then let's press on in prayer, faith and doctrine for the other two! The term "ascension" is borrowed from the fact that as Christ arose He gave these gifts to The Body. In the same way that The HOLY SPIRIT gives spiritual gifts[21] and The FATHER[22] appoints men into office and

[21] 1Corinthians 12:11
[22] 1Corinthians 12:18, 28

position so The LORD Jesus[23] gives these gifts to His Church.

Now yes, the terms 'prophet' and 'apostle' seem to be very ambiguous and raise all sorts of questions right now. Part of this is that many of us have had our fingers burnt with those who are either immature or have otherwise tainted our perception in a negative way. But may I suggest that for every false or immature item there is a mature and true original? True, we hardly know what they are or what they're meant to do. But certainly we should not be nervous or cowed about discussing them and being open to GOD on the matter. Let's bear in mind: a) GOD who may still be appointing[24] them to help us! b) The process of restoration back to the 1st century apostolic church that began on that church door in Wittenberg in 1517[25] may still be continuing in 2011 . . . . Hummm . . ?

Equipping gifts

Each of the gifts when properly released in a congregation infuses everyone with their particular grace, passion, worldview and gifting. So if a church is exposed to an evangelist the congregants will likely be 'evangelistic' - the verb form, and so

---

[23] Ephesians 4:11
[24] 1Cornithians 12:28
[25] Date of Martin Luther's 95 Thesis sparking the 1st reformation

on for all the 5-fold gifts. To 'equip the saints for the work of the ministry[26].

Maybe, just maybe we should be looking in the future at having prophetic and even apostolic churches? But WHO will equip them?

Perhaps we need some unabashed 'nouns' rather than 'adjectives' to step forward? People who will receive the title not just say they are being '_ _ _ _ _ -tic'

---

[26] Ephesians 4:12

SO, IS THERE ROOM FOR MORE?

Come along with me on this thought process; If we seek to build His Kingdom primarily on these three ministry gifts what will church look like and what impact will it have on society?

To help with this we can if you'll come along with me look at two present day scenarios, one in my native Nigeria, and the other in my adopted homeland of Kent, UK. Starting with Nigeria, a nation awash with pastors, evangelists and teachers . . Let's see if this mix of ministry gifts has so far, by itself, been successful in bringing The Kingdom of Heaven[27] down to Earth?

But first I have a poser for us: What's the big deal with apostles?

Why did Paul have to go on and on about verifying his apostleship? (1Corinthians 9:1-2) What was the big issue? What was it with this term apostle? Why the warnings against false apostles? Why did The LORD commend the Ephesians for exposing false apostles? (Rev 2:2) We could have made demands on you as apostles said Paul, 'as apostles', (1Thess 2:6) there's that term again. What was so special? It seems that the 1st century church was blitzed with apostles. 'They met with the apostles and elders

---

[27] Matthew 11:2

74

and the whole church' (Acts 15:4) who were these mystery men that went by the title 'apostle'? Yet stood apart from the 'elders'? Why did Paul begin most of his letters with the preface, 'Paul an apostle'? We can take it as a given that he wasn't being arrogant. So what was it that made this claim to this position so pertinent? Paul writes in his, 'say hello section' about a couple of guys who were 'of note among the apostles', yet apart from here we never hear of them. (Romans 16:7) Who were this mystery group of people that were so accepted in the culture of the early church? Name, title and all?

CHURCH IN NIGERIA

In Nigeria in most towns across the southeast and southwest we have a scenario of churches on every street corner, evangelists holding weekly campaigns and cassette tapes of street hawkers broadcasting messages from popular teachers. But despite all of this the towns do not yet have a Christian ethos, crime is still rampant and the civil service largely under-performing. This leads us to ask the following questions: -

a) Has the governmental church system in place that has released literally scores of thousands of pastors and evangelists turned Nigeria into a Christian nation?

b) Have the largest church buildings in the world and monthly prayer meetings in excess of a million people so far succeeded in bringing The Kingdom of Heaven down to Earth in the most populous black nation on Earth?

NO, NOT YET - But the Church is waiting for something, The Kingdom of GOD stands poised, expectant, something more is about to be released on the church. It will equip the saints to win the kingdoms of this world for our GOD!!

So, what's missing? What's not happening?

Two things: -

a. The government of the gospel or kingdom of GOD must be effectively introduced to challenge and transform the predominant worldly culture and mindset of the day from 'pagan materialism' to 'kingdom righteousness'.

b.   Order must be brought in the realm of the spirit. This is where battles for peoples and nations are fought and won. Any disorder will be in part due to a reflection of the lack of order in The Church and a symptom of dysfunctional church governing paradigms. Paul said of the church in Colossae[28], 'I rejoice to see your order in the spirit' where the order was self evident and clear in the spirit realm. Part of Titus' mandate in Crete was to set things in order[29]

Statement (a) raises the question, "Who will take the gospel of the kingdom (not just that of salvation) out from the confines of the church into the yet to be reached sections of society and the marketplace (the world system)?" It is by this osmotic process that our salt (in which the culture of The Kingdom is contained) is infused into the world around us.

Statement (b) raises the questions, "Who will order the troops for battle?" "Who will bring unity to the fractured Body of Christ?" Without this unity the church will run in circles and quickly quench and abort the many moves of GOD our beloved intercessors stir heaven to release. The unity we speak of here is of the spirit, (Ephesians 4:3) which we are instructed to walk in now!

---

[28] Colossians 2:15
[29] Titus 1:5

The unity of the faith (Ephesians 4:13) will come as we press on with all the 5-fold giftings restored.

THE APOSTLE

As we are probably aware, the term apostle did not have its origins in the religious world, rather it was imported from the use of the day. In the days of the early church it was a term for a high-ranking Roman delegate sent and empowered by the emperor to establish the rule, culture and traditions of Rome in annexed territories of the world. The Greek term apostolos is derived from the word, sent. So a predominant aspect of an apostolic call is a strong awareness of being sent.

The HOLY SPIRIT is 'released' through the ministry of the apostle

From a glance through the Acts of the Apostles we see that the apostles were key to more of The SPIRIT being 'released' on Earth. Starting in Jerusalem[30], being repeated later on in Jerusalem[31], then in Samaria[32] followed by Caesarea[33], then onto Ephesus[34] - in each place the primary mission of the apostles was to release a fresh outbreak of The HOLY SPIRIT in that town and region.

---

[30] Acts 2:2
[31] Acts 4:31
[32] Acts 8:14,15
[33] Acts 10:44
[34] Acts 19:6

78

DEFINING APOSTLES

Here is a description of the ministry gift of apostle stemming from my observations of church culture in Asia, America, Europe and Africa as well as what I have gleaned from the writings of others mentioned earlier on.

1. Someone charged with taking the Gospel of The Kingdom out of the "four walls of the church" (an established community of faith) and introducing it to society. This usually entails: -

   a. Coalescing a team for a fresh groundbreaking church plant that gathers momentum and progresses into a movement of new communities of believers - churches. (Acts 13:4, 14:14).

   b. Facilitating a network of church and ministry leaders to effectively 'take their cities for GOD' resulting in community transformation.

   c. Receiving and implementing an effective blue print for sustained and systematic church growth. (1Corinthians 3:10; Ephesians 2:20)

d.   Being called and equipped to 'possess a mountain' of influence in society for The Kingdom of GOD.

2.   A 'father figure', who brings, maintains, strives for and eventually symbolises unity (Galatians 2:9), order (Titus 1:5) and reconciliation (Acts 15:2) to a cross section of The Body of Christ. This is usually within a particular denominational movement or a clear-cut geo-political or cultural setting (Galatians 2:8).

3.   A minister who is graced (1Corinthians 15:10) to accomplish the previous two items by a marked degree of transferable power and delegated authority. (Matthew 10:1,2; Acts 4:33; 5:12) For a 'church apostle' this would be demonstrated in spiritual signs and wonders resulting from manifestations of gifts of The Holy Spirit. For the 'marketplace apostle' (Definition of this term below) this would be in terms of rank and status acquired in their sphere of operation.

Questions?

a. Firstly weren't there just twelve and didn't they die out with the early church?

Actually there were twelve initially but this group grew and there were up to sixteen more referred to in the epistles: -

Matthias (Acts 1:26); Paul (1 Corinthians 15:8) James the brother of Jesus (Gal. 1:19); Barnabas (Acts 14:3,4,14); Apollos (1Cor 4:6-9); Timothy (Acts 19:22: 1 Thessalonians 1:1: 2:6); Titus (2 Cor 8:23 where "messenger" is apostolos); Silas (Acts 15:22, 1Thess 1:1; 2:6); Tychicus (2 Tim. 4:12); Judas (Acts 15:22; 1 Thess. 2:6); Andronicus (Rom. 16:7); Junia (whose name indicates this might have been a woman), (Rom. 16:7; Epaphroditus Phil. 2:25); Erastus (Acts 19:22); and two unnamed apostles (2 Cor. 8:23).

Clearly, if only the twelve were apostles then it would not have made any sense for Paul to warn against "false apostles" (2Corinthians 11:13) or The LORD to commend the church in Ephesus for finding certain apostles to be false (Rev 2:2)

Further, Paul refers to the LORD as being seen alive by "Peter and the twelve" and then by "James and all the apostles" (1Corinth 15:5,7), the James here referred was not the James who was part of the original twelve (Acts12:2) but the half brother of Jesus. The "apostles" here refers to a different group.

As to whether they died out with the early church - yes they largely did! But so did miracles, signs and wonders and a victorious advancing church! What may perhaps be more pertinent to prayerfully petition is?

Father-GOD was it Your intent that the church advance no farther, being hamstrung by the absence of these gifts? Or have we been in continuous reformation and restoration of church? Taking us back to the life, passion, power and sacrifice of the early church?"

This would include such items as justification by faith, empowering the laity, the right of every believer to have access to the scriptures, baptism as an expression of faith, healing being a blessing from GOD etc etc..

b. Aren't apostles church planters who move about from place to place?

Not necessarily so, we've known teachers who start churches by holding a seminar on some 'hot' topic and through this attract people, ditto for pastors who start as home groups offering love and care to people, evangelists too who win souls through being out there in the community and have been known to start churches.

Typically apostles start churches by birthing a movement, through a powerful influx of The SPIRIT. From this movement men and women are then sent out in the power of The Spirit so generated. The vital ingredient to new churches is not the apostles' mobility but the transferable grace and anointing that is transmitted to those in voluntary relationship and submission to them. Hence although Paul fulfilled his ministry through a great deal of travel, other apostles like Peter and James operated primarily from a base in Jerusalem (Galatians 1:18,19; Acts 8:1; 15:2)

c. Aren't missionaries apostles?

These two terms aren't to be confused. Peter was described as an apostle to the Jews, yet he was also a Jew (Galatians 2:8), so no cross-cultural gift was required. A missionary is someone with a grace to work in another cultural setting with a knack of being able to contextualise the kingdom message. Paul, a Jew had this grace (Ephesians 3:8) whereas Peter didn't (Galatians 2:11-14). Any ministry gift may be hyphenated with a missionary mix added on e.g. missionary pastor.

Here are a few more posers to help with the question, "Are apostles for the 21st century?"

Q1. Have We Seen Any Apostles In The Last Few Decades?

I believe that Christianity would not be where it is today if we had not had numerous apostles. However, even in the charismatic circles of Nigeria talk less of a more conservative UK we have been, by and large coy about this nomenclature. Perhaps for fear of offending long standing tradition perhaps?

83

1930-2000
In recent times apostles pioneered the modern day (and presently reforming) charismatic movement.

They were backed by the charismata (graces from the Spirit of GOD), which initially drew in scores of disciples. The resultant culture of unity, love and voluntary submission of these ones brought in more of The SPIRIT and released more charismata on the emerging leaders of these movements. This spawned a church planting movement right across the nations of the world, which continues today.

1850 - 1930
Historically, many mainline denominations were started by apostles. These denominations started out as groundbreaking moves of GOD leading to their becoming 'movements' before eventually becoming 'denominations' in the passage of time. We can think of The Wesley brothers' – Methodism and William Booth – The Salvation Army Church, Aimee Semple McPherson – The Foursquare Gospel Church, Charles Parham – The

Assemblies of GOD, in Nigeria we have many notable denominations all similarly started by apostles although they have rarely up until now gone by that name.

These pioneers had and have grace to: -

a.   Instigate a fresh release of The HOLY SPIRIT.

b.   Draw large crowds of people into The Kingdom.

c.   Form new wine skins that would be well adapted to the resulting attendant new spiritual norms and nuances of faith.

Q2. Who Are Marketplace Apostles?

The marketplace apostle works through the position of influence that they occupy in the world system (e.g. Banker, Politician, Educator, Sportsperson etc). They see themselves as representatives of The Kingdom of GOD and war to see godly values defended, entrenched or re-affirmed in the setting that they are called to. It is my joy to know several apostles across Nigeria as well as in the UK who are called to the business community, the police force, the medical community, the entertainment world as well as the political world. And the list is growing!

There is a huge difference between for example, a politician who happens to be a Christian on the one hand and a Christian who has been called, commissioned and sent into the political sphere and sees this as a divine calling to rule, reign and 'occupy' that territory for GOD. (e.g. Joseph, Daniel)

Q3. Are Apostles 'All Powerful' In Their Use Of Authority? (Apostolic Spheres)

Apostles all have clear and well-defined spheres of influence (2Corinthians 10:13) - boundaries beyond which they are unable to function as they are out of jurisdiction.

This is significant because it lets us know that an apostle is limited or empowered in his or her effectiveness by the strength and trust of existing relationships. Where there is no relationship an apostle has no function.

Q4. What Will Be The Key Differences In Immediate Past Apostolic Ministry And Emerging 21st Century Apostles?

As part of the ongoing reformation and restoration of the ministry gifts a massive fresh wave of apostles is being commissioned and released from heaven. They will continue the work of earlier apostles in accomplishing all three of the things done previously as well as reintroducing several features unique to apostles that for the most part are yet to be restored.

To understand one of these aspects, we see that 20th century apostles have given rise to a global church planting movement headed primarily by pastors and evangelists who have a primary focus of getting people saved and added to the church.

The new tier 21st century apostles however, are being equipped with a much wider commission. They don't just want new churches, they want the land transformed and the His rule in every aspect of society!

They want justice in the law courts, equity in the economy, healing and deliverance in the prisons, righteousness in the schools, safety on the streets and The Kingdom in our homes.

What will be the key differences in modus operandi between the two groups?

> 1.   New levels of grace in humility, submission, interdependence and accountability will forge these ministers together into apostolic covenants, roundtables and councils similar to that seen in Acts 13 & 15. Grace to sustain and perpetuate regional REVIVAL FIRE will come from these powerful servant councils.

> 2.   These apostolic councils will not be confined to or restricted by different movements and factions of The Body, but will seek to blanket the earth in fulfilment of the great commission as they covenant with, and hold allegiance to specific geographical regions / sub sections of society.

3.   The new apostles will walk in tandem with another emerging ministry gift resulting in exponential increases in demonstrations of power and wisdom, signs and wonders on the Earth.

Apostles in the 21st century and beyond: So, is there room? Is there a need?

Have we got faith that The FATHER still desires to release many more moves of The HOLY SPIRIT to our towns and neighbourhoods? Do we still believe that our nation can turn to GOD en masse as it has done in the past?

- As happened in the Wesleyan revivals when a whole load of worship melodies was forever etched into the hearts and minds of an entire generation?

- As happened in the Babalola Revival in Nigeria in the 1930's when the destiny of the Yoruba people was forever transformed by the preaching of an illiterate steamroller driver and his followers?

- As in the days of the 2nd Great Awakening when whole cities in America came to a standstill to hear and respond to the preaching of Charles Finney?

Then let's believe GOD together for the generation in which we live to be impacted by hundreds of thousands of these Miracle, Sign & Wonder workers - a new day in GOD's calendar dawns upon us, it's time for a fresh apostolic age! "COME LORD JESUS! RELEASE YOUR GIFT OF APOSTLE ON YOUR CHURCH ONCE MORE!"

Apostles – who on earth needs them?

CHAPTER 6
Prophets & Prophetic people

"How that by revelation He made known to me the
mystery (as I have briefly written already, by
which, when you read, you may understand my
knowledge in the mystery of Christ), which in
other ages was not made known to the sons of men,
as it has now been revealed by the Spirit to His
holy apostles and prophets"
Ephesians 3:3-5

'DON'T BE AFRAID'

. . the prophet answered. "Those who are with us are more than those who are with them." And Elisha prayed, "Open his eyes, LORD, so that he may see." Then the LORD opened the servant's eyes, and he looked and saw the hills full of horses and chariots of fire all around Elisha. As the enemy came down toward him, Elisha prayed to the LORD, "Strike this army with blindness." So he struck them with blindness, as Elisha had asked. . . After they entered the city, Elisha said, "LORD, open the eyes of these men so they can see." Then the LORD opened their eyes and they looked, and there they were, inside Samaria. When the king of Israel saw them, he asked Elisha, "Shall I kill them, my father? Shall I kill them?" "Do not kill them," he answered. "Would you kill those you have captured with your own sword or bow? Set food and water before them so that they may eat and drink and then go back to their master." . . . and they returned to their master. So the bands from Aram stopped raiding Israel's territory"
(2Kings 6:16-18)

Those called to the same ministry as E-L-I-S-H-A: -

1. <u>E-</u> ffectively war in the spiritual realm to restore peace to the Earth.
2. <u>L-</u> ive to serve others
3. <u>I-</u> ntimately can connect with heaven
4. <u>S-</u> ee into the spiritual realm.
5. <u>H-</u> elp others to also see
6. <u>A-</u> re merciful

CHURCH IN KENT, ENGLAND

In continuing to look at the question, **"Apostles and Prophets - Who on earth needs them?"** I'd like to take a look at the church scene in my adopted homeland of Kent. We'll start with a few case notes from happenings in and around Whitstable, where I live: -

Case 1:
A couple of years ago meetings were going on in a town in the area where a nightly outpouring of The Spirit of GOD was occurring. GOD's Presence was tangible, miracles were happening, and people were getting touched by The LORD. A dear brother had attended these meetings to seek more of GOD. During the worship time, he had seen what looked like a ball of fire hurtling towards him. As it hit him, he was struck down to the ground. He didn't know what to make of this fireball; was this

experience from GOD or the enemy? He had not been 'baptised in The Spirit' and had no prior knowledge of such powerful supernatural outworkings. Confusion set in followed by depression. He was not able to accept this experience as from The LORD.

Comment:
Unusual powerful demonstrations of The Spirit of GOD always need to be judged, explained, monitored and interpreted. Especially in highly charged spiritual environments clear prophetic protocols must kick in to avoid confusion. The brother in question did not take counsel from someone who had been exposed to such occurrences and who offered insight into what had happened. It is open to discussion how well the church leadership had prepared people for what may take place in these meetings. (1Thess 5:19-21).

Case 2:
It was a powerful meeting, again in a nearby town. Heartfelt prayer was made by those who took the microphone that this would be a night of revival, of outpouring of GOD's Spirit. The worship leader rose to the occasion, The Presence of GOD was rich and inviting. A known leader rose to ask to release a prophetic word that had risen in his heart, with a view to release more of what was being poured out from heaven.

Sadly the convenor of the meeting shied away from this and chose to return the event back into a much safer structured event. Worshippers who were sprawled on the floor in surrender to GOD had this flow of 'spiritual oxygen' suddenly cut off. We had a program to work through.

Comment:
Often when we pray for revival we fail to take into account that this means allowing GOD's Spirit to 'wreck' our meeting as we submit to His plans and outpouring! Outpourings are seldom neat, tidy and structured. We are given a choice to flow with HIS will or wrest control of the meeting back from HIM.

Case 3:
A minister visited a church in a nearby town for a conference by a high profile speaker; as the worship went on it was as if the worship was bouncing back off the ceiling! As he sat there his spiritual eyes were opened to see that this was not an acoustics issue but a spiritual one. The host minister was approached who readily acknowledged the feeling of 'oppression'.

Comment:
Sadly although help and testimony of deliverance in similar situations was offered this was not received.

Case 4:
For two previous years the minister had seen a manifestation of GOD's Glory at the same time in the month as this year. His heart beat in expectation of what would come at this particular service in a nearby town. As the worship began GOD's Presence was tangible. You could almost swim in it, it was so thick. He began to perceive a

mighty manifestation of The Presence of GOD descending on the congregation . . then suddenly this beautiful flow stopped! Someone who was inexperienced had taken the mic and grieved The SPIRIT! That was it; the time of heavenly visitation had been stopped and was not to be retrieved again.

Comment:
Many times we are required to by our actions respond to the question, "Can we trust The HOLY SPIRIT to do more with the meeting than we had planned to by ourselves? We always have a choice in the matter, to flow with The SPIRIT or to wrest the meeting back to our original intent. "Do not quench The SPIRIT" we are enjoined. (1Thess 5:19) Don't grieve HIM (Eph4:13)

Case 5:
A minister was engrossed in an avid discussion with a member of his church who seemed to have some odd beliefs.

In mid sentence the church member began to prophesy to himself, putting his own name in the prophecy! The prophetic word was given to corroborate his own views as opposed to what his minister was trying to tell him. Dumbfounded the minister walked away. The man he had been seeking to help often had prophetic words for the congregation, now he was trying to use his gift to get a personal word from The LORD in a bid to back his personal viewpoint!

Comment:
You can't deliver a personal word of prophecy to yourself in a bid to defend yourself or win an argument! This leads to manipulation and in the extremity, witchcraft.

Case 6:
A member of a church in the area had a prophetic word for his leaders. It was a directional and cautionary word and they wondered what to do with it. They did not feel they could just abandon it and were desirous to not quench the spirit. They needed someone to come alongside them to sort through the procedure of dealing with this prophetic word.

Comment:
A minister came along and based on what he said, they felt comfortable that if GOD wanted to speak to them it would come through those in relational leadership with them and would be confirmed by more than one source. At the mouth of two or three witnesses everything be established. (2Corinthians 13:1). They could leave the word to one side knowing they were not guilty of despising prophecy.

Case 7:
"Aren't tongues for use in preaching to foreign tribes?" The dear enquirer asked the minister. "I think tongues are mainly for worship" offered another. "So many times people have prayed for me to speak in tongues and nothings happened" said one more. Ten minutes later she was speaking away in tongues with great joy!

Comment:
'Tongues' aka 'prayer in the spirit' is really such basic gift, yet because of lack of understanding so many are deprived of the benefits of it. A particular ministry is empowered by grace to equip the saints with supernatural spiritual gifts.

Time now to look at this ministry gift and bring out its primary functions: -

Description of the MINISTRY GIFT OF PROPHET

This person is primarily concerned with what is going on in the spirit realm. They are involved in prayer, in bringing prophetic words, in deliverance ministry and in generally discerning what FATHER

may be saying to The Body. They are sensitive to the spiritual realm.

They carry an above average sense of what The SPIRIT is saying. On various levels of operation

they are like the sons of Issachar who knew what time it was and what Israel ought to do (1Chronicles 12:32)

Without this gift in operation we are restricted in accurately discerning spiritual manifestations. We may be left unsure if a word is from the HOLY SPIRIT, the enemy, the flesh or a mixing of all. (Acts 16:16-18). To assist him (or her) with this process, the prophet will have one or more spiritual revelatory gifts in operation (Word of Knowledge, Word of Wisdom, Discerning of spirits - 1Corinthians 12:8-10). These gifts help him to discern WHAT IS GOING ON? And who is behind it?

Without the prophets the rest of us are often scared stiff of all this super-spiritual stuff. Scared and intimidated. Our attitudes that have been shaped by stories of things going adrift, of those who have used prophetic utterances to manipulate situations make us nervous of prophecy and the supernatural. Not surprisingly we shut any such odd behaviour down! "Not on my watch!" we say. Without putting it into so many words we'd usually rather have nothing going on and maintain order than dare to try to have all things going on and struggle with trying to maintain order. We deem it too risky to have prophetic words, tongues and people with visions demanding our attention. (1Corinth 14:40)

WHAT DO PROPHETS AND PROPHETIC PEOPLE DO?

1. They strengthen and encourage the work of GOD. This is through instilling hope, faith and vision by virtue of their prophetic gift.

    And the elders of the Jews built, and they prospered through the prophesying of Haggai the prophet and Zechariah the son of Iddo. (Ezra 6:14)

    "But the one who prophesies speaks to people for their strengthening, encouraging and comfort" (1Cornithians 14:3)

2. They interpret what is going on in the spiritual realm so that The Church can capitalise on this by acting accordingly. (2Kings 6:16-18)

3. When they minister they carry with them and release a prophetic environment making the giving and releasing of the gift of prophecy available to those around them.

    Word came to Saul: "David is in Naioth at Ramah"; so he sent men to capture him. But when they saw a group of prophets prophesying, with Samuel standing there as their leader, the Spirit of God came on Saul's men, and they also prophesied. Saul was told about it, and he sent more men, and they prophesied too. Saul sent men a third time, and they also prophesied. (1Samuel 19:19-21)

4. Prophetic encounters dispel fear and suspicion; of what might be, of the enemy, of the supernatural, of the unknown. Some years back my mother; a believer at the time had a dream about her beloved aunt. In the dream she saw angels carrying her off from her bed. The next day this was no small comfort to her on hearing the news that her she had died the previous night.

Similarly, my Dad tells the story of the last hour of his beloved uncle. His uncle realising that he was about to breath his last, called all his relatives to his bedside. After dividing his possessions among them and stating his last will, he began to cry out for joy, "The angels are here, the angels are here" in his native Yoruba tongue, he asked if those around him could hear the sounds of singing? With his arms spread out, he breathed his last. Needless to say the funeral was one of joy and fanfare. Let's not be afraid of supernatural manifestations. Paul wrote, concerning spiritual gifts, 'I don't want you ignorant or misinformed' (1Corinthians 12:1)

5. Those called to prophetic office judge and interpret prophetic words, signs and spiritual manifestations; they unravel anything that appears 'spooky'. Yes, the enemy will try to get in if we are ignorant and misinformed. That's why prophets, teachers and prophetic people are needed - to introduce us to the bounty of our inheritance as believers in the spiritual realm.

    "Do not quench the Spirit. Do not treat prophecies with contempt but test them all; hold on to what is good" (1Thess 5: 19-21)

"Two or three prophets should speak, and the others should weigh carefully what is said" (1Corithians 14:29)

6. Based on what they see or perceive through the spiritual gifts they have been equipped with they are able to carry out deliverance by expelling demonic forces from people and 'haunted' houses.

   Once when we were going to the place of prayer, we were met by a female slave who had a spirit by which she predicted the future. She earned a great deal of money for her owners by fortune telling. She followed Paul and the rest of us,

   shouting, "These men are servants of the Most High God, who are telling you the way to be saved." She kept this up for many days. Finally Paul became so annoyed that he turned around and said to the spirit, "In the name of Jesus Christ I command you to come out of her!" At that moment the spirit left her.
   (Acts 16:16-18)

7. They equip the saints to do the work of ministry. This is by imparting the spiritual gifts that they walk in to other believers. From the most elementary gifts like tongues, interpretation of tongues and prophesy to more advanced gifts like discerning of

spirits, word of knowledge etc. When any Ephesians 4 ministry gift is in place and received it imparts part of that same grace to the local company of believers. (Ephesians 4:11-13; Romans 1:11)

OLD TESTAMENT cf. NEW TESTAMENT PROPHETS

A word here about a major difference between prophets in the Old Testament and the New Testament: -

OT Prophets came 'ready-to-go'. Consequently a prophet in the OT could be judged false if his words were not 'spot-on'.

NT Prophets however take years of refining before they get it all right. Room is given for their words

to not be 100%. As a prophetic friend put it, ministering in the prophetic is more art than science in the NT. We are enjoined to prophecy according to our faith. (Romans 12:6) This is why procedure is put in place that sieves prophetic words for accuracy, why scriptures are replete with instruction to test prophecy. For the NT Prophet much practise and maturing is needed to get it all right. I personally believe that even then we still get words wrong as a way of keeping us humble and dependent on one another!

True or false prophet?

The test for whether a prophet is true or false is reflected in the state of their heart towards GOD and the people they are called to serve; their motivations for ministry. The OT Prophet Balaam who gave true prophetic words is considered a false prophet not because his prophecies were false but because his motives were wrong. (2Peter 2:14-16 and Revelation 2:14)

SO, WHO ON EARTH NEEDS THEM?

Prophets and prophetic people . . . how far can we go without them?

They carry keys to unlock mysteries, they open the supernatural realm to us, they **empower us** to give prophetic words, they unlock the destinies of men, peoples and nations. They are Christ's ascension gift to us, HIS Church.

OK to be fair, they come with a fair share of problems, true. So next week we will look at the maturing process that those called to apostolic and prophetic ministry are most often required to submit to. And why they usually require a greater schooling process than pastors, evangelists, administrators and teachers.

We'll also look at how (for those of us how are up for it!) we can gingerly begin to incorporate them into our church systems.

CHAPTER 7
PEALS OF THUNDER

"Then there came flashes of lightning, rumblings, peals of thunder and a severe earthquake. No earthquake like it has ever occurred since man has been on earth, so tremendous was the quake."
Revelation 16:18

"PEALS OF THUNDER"

Definition (Peal): -
A ringing of a set of bells, <u>especially a change or set of changes</u> rung on bells.

QUAKES in Church Government

As we enter into the second decade of the 21st century an emerging apostolic and prophetic movement is about being thrust into significance on a global scale. In preparation for this men and women are being drafted into position to form networks or wineskins that will catch the wind and wave of first RENEWAL, then REVIVAL then REFORMATION as gifts, graces, signs and wonders on both the earth as well as in the heavens are released. There will be geographical apparitions and spectacular displays in nature, as Creation itself can't hold back from the excitement of the hour!

I write this, as much to signal The Body to prepare itself as well as to call to The Church to re-align relationally with what is the stirring in her heart for 'The New'. This 'New' will be radical in its outlook, as radical as things must have been for the reformers of the 1700 and 1800's. The inclusion of the apostolic and prophetic graces in church government will cause an explosion in old staid concepts of church and how churches run.

Multitudes of new churches and expressions of church will arise within a few short years of this new move being triggered. In this last section we address the issue of, 'How do we assimilate emerging apostles & prophets into present church structure?'

However we need to stand this question on its head. For the genuine prophet and apostle it will not to be as much a question of, 'How do we assimilate them into our churches?' as 'How do they assimilate us? - i.e. into the new government that they are being called to, released in and empowered in (as The Kingdom of GOD is released and expanded on Earth through their ministries).

For centuries the church has been built on a governmental structure of pastors and administrators. The coming REFORMATION and realignment of government is about a totally new Wine Skin and system of church government. It will be an upheaval of the way the vast majority of us have done church for most of our lives.

The thing is, looking back at things over the last few decades we've seen ministry gifts of pastor, evangelist and teacher as well as others being restored back into church systems with varying degrees of success. One may have assumed that as reformation continued that apostles as well as prophets would similarly be welcomed then, integrated. The error in this thinking is that apostles and prophets however are (by the very

definition of their function) <u>foundational</u> in church government! This being so, then clearly things will not work for them to be integrated into our system - this would defeat half of the purpose for which they are being restored - to bring us back to biblical, straight-line apostolic government! Wow! Do you see it with me?! This is so powerful in its ramifications for what is on the spiritual horizon!

WHAT NEXT?

So, as leaders what does this mean on a practical, down to earth level?

I believe an answer is found in a word play of **"P - E - A - L"**

1. **P** - pray for: -
   a. The emergence of the apostolic and prophetic vessels in your area. Pray them 'out of the woodwork'. Many are insecure and wounded from being sidelined for most of their years in church. Pray love, strength and courage on them.
   b. The healing and eventual maturing of those with a call to be prophets or apostles. 'Issues' need to be delved into. Half-buried, subconscious traits

and paradigms often toxic in nature and detrimental to the preservation of The New Wine need to be exposed, healed and resolved.

c. A realigning of 'dislocated' prophets and apostles and a 'setting' back into The Body of Christ.

d. The amalgamation of (strongly relational) apostolic and prophetic roundtables in your area.

2. **E** - earnestly seek: -

a. Guidance in commencing / continuing / rekindling (as the case may be) of relationship with those who have apostolic or prophetic grace on their lives.

b. Grace to adopt a heart attitude of humility and yieldedness to the will of GOD especially in terms of governmental authority and positioning.

NB. We need to ensure that we are free from a heart of 'ownership' of, or marriage to, The Bride - The Body of Christ is not our wife, we are merely called to prepare Her for marriage to another - The LORD JESUS!

3. **A** - align with and encourage meetings that are of a prophetic nature. The LORD wants to speak loudly into our midst. We can facilitate this sort of gathering by holding

extended worship meetings (emphasis on 'worship' cf 'prayer'). Let the agenda of these meetings be strictly to seek HIM and hear from HIM. A vital yet overlooked by-product of this sort of meeting is the releasing of tangible (though invisible) grace for the journey.

4. **L** - look for (and apply) the plumb-line of character and fruit of The SPIRIT to those who are at the forefront of prophetic and apostolic activity in your vicinity. This will ascertain either their preparedness for service presently or (regrettably) the need for further maturing until later. The fruits of gentleness, love, perseverance and deadness to self are ('LORD, be merciful') non negotiable in the very sensitive and imminent transition from pastoral to apostolic government.

REFLECTIONS . . . .

A prayer to receive JESUS as your LORD and SAVIOUR

Dear LORD JESUS,
I believe that you died on the cross for me. I believe that you died in my place for all my sins, all that I have done wrong. I thank You that You loved me enough to give Your life as a sacrifice for mine. I receive your love for me right now; I ask that you take away my sins and all that has been wrong in my life. Please wash me clean and come to live in my heart. I accept you as my LORD and Saviour. Thank you for saving me, for coming into my heart and life. I love you and receive the eternal life that You give right now. Thank You LORD JESUS! Amen.

A prayer to receive the baptism of The HOLY SPIRIT and His gifts

Dear FATHER-GOD,
I thank you for sending JESUS I have received as my LORD and Saviour. Thank You that I now qualify for Your promise to also me to be filled with the power of The HOLY SPIRIT. I come to You on the basis of Your Word, the Bible and right now ask You to fill me, drench me and flood me to overflowing with Your precious gift of the HOLY SPIRIT. HOLY SPIRIT I receive You into my life now in a unique, personal, powerful and special way. Thank You as You fill me, for the gifts You also have to give me especially the divine ability to

speak in other tongues and prophecy. I ask for and believe You for these gifts to show up in my life right away! Thank You my FATHER! Thank You LORD JESUS! Thank You precious and dear HOLY SPIRIT! Amen.

Other books by the same author -

1. **LEST WE FORGET** – The life and times of the pioneer missionaries to Ibadan, Nigeria (1851 – 1868) As a young girl Anna's dream was to one day be a martyr for JESUS. This is the powerful story of her life along with her husband David, who were the first Christian missionaries to Ibadan in southwest Nigeria from 1851 to 1868. As you read it you will be impacted by a life on fire for GOD!

2. **THE WELLS OF OUR FATHERS** - A history of revival in southwest Nigeria from 1830 to 1959. But this is far more than a history lesson, this is about honouring the lives of all who have gone before us and laid foundations. It is on these foundations that we stand and ascend to the next levels of faith and reformation that The HOLY SPIRIT has in store for us. Life and grace are released as we honour these generals, prophets and apostles who have preceded us. We owe them.

3. **TRANSITION** – Something new is on the horizon! Highlighting areas that The HOLY SPIRIT is revealing to His saints where emphasis and change are needed to break old moulds and be supple to be able to contain the new wine falling on the church. This book starts off with a list of 25 such

116

areas then hones in on six of them including restoration of the prophetic and apostolic offices.

4. **CROSSOVER!** – A manual for transcending societal & cultural obstacles for maximum impact. This book is a reminder of the love The FATHER has for the cultures and nations of the world. Featuring practical ways for social contextulisation including how to conduct socially open church services and contemporary evangelistic paradigms. The FATHER's love is portrayed for us as individuals freeing us to our unique and precious identities.

5. **YOU CAN PROPHESY! 70 truths about the gift of prophecy** - A handy and concise resource covering 22 Reasons to Prophesy, 7 Ways to Prepare for Prophetic Words and Encounters, 7 Ways to Activate Prophetic Grace and loads more. This book presents prophesy as a gift available to every believer, it is not a mark of some great level or height of spirituality.

6. **TRAINING & ACTIVATION MANUALS** – Equipping the saints (Ephesians 4:11) - Three resources for training in all righteousness that the man of GOD may be fully equipped in primary areas of the faith. – Equipping the saints (Ephesians 4:11)

a. **25 types of Prayer, Tongues and Interpretation** – all in one manual. LORD teach us to pray was the cry of the disciples, 'LORD make it ours too!'

b. **Prophecy and Prophetic evangelism** – this gift belongs to us! It is not just for the super saint! Covering all the basics you need to walk in prophecy as your spiritual inheritance.

c. **Faith, Working Of Miracles & Gifts Of Healings** – 21 ways GOD heals today!

ABOUT

Robin and Nyema are "return missionaries" to the UK having received a vision for missions mobilisation in July 1996 in Ibadan, Nigeria. They lead "Servant Ministries", an equipping ministry to The Body through itinerant ministry, book writing and seminars. They also lead "The Whitstable Tabernacle" a regular gathering for prayer, worship and release of the prophetic. They convene the "Inter-Prophetic Alliance", a relational gathering of heads of prayer and prophetic ministries.

Robin, a Nigerian Englishman is the author of "TRANSITION - *a compass for shifting from the old to the new featuring key areas of reformation for the post-charismatic kingdom saint*", as well as several manuals on prophetic ministry and books on revival.

Servant Ministries is aligned with "Churches in Communities", an international grouping of minsters under Dr Hugh Osgood, Robin is ordained as a prophet under "Christian International Europe" (CIE), led by Dr Sharon Stone and has as his mentor Bishop Joe Ibojie of The Father's House", Aberdeen, he is a spiritual son of Apostle Mosy Madugba of Ministers Prayer Network. Nyema is a worshipper and prophetic intercessor and is passionate to see healings, signs and wonders on the earth. Robin and Nyema are part of The Harbour Church, Whitstable. They are blessed with four children, a nephew and a niece and make their home in Whitstable, Kent.

TRANSITION

Printed in Poland
by Amazon Fulfillment
Poland Sp. z o.o., Wrocław

54863466R00078